Effective Self-Care and Resilience in Clinical Practice

of related interest

Mindfulness for Carers
How to Manage the Demands of Caregiving
While Finding a Place for Yourself
Dr Cheryl Rezek
ISBN 978 1 84905 654 0
eISBN 978 1 78450 147 1

Being Mindful, Easing Suffering
Reflections of Palliative Care
Christopher Johns
ISBN 978 1 84310 212 0
eISBN 978 1 84642 028 3

Emerging Values in Health Care
The Challenge for Professionals
Edited by Stephen Pattison, Ben Hannigan, Roisin Pill and Huw Thomas
ISBN 978 1 84310 947 1
eISBN 978 0 85700 365 2

Hope and Grace
Spiritual Experiences in Severe Distress, Illness and Dying
Dr Monika Renz
ISBN 978 1 78592 030 1   ·
eISBN 978 1 78450 277 5

Effective Self-Care and Resilience in Clinical Practice

Dealing with Stress, Compassion Fatigue and Burnout

Edited by Dr SARAH PARRY, ClinPsyD

Foreword by PAUL GILBERT, PhD, FBPsS, OBE

Jessica Kingsley *Publishers*
London and Philadelphia

den Heijer quote on p.75 reproduced with kind permission of Alexander den Heijer.
Watson quote on p.90 reproduced with kind permission of Dr Jean Watson.

First published in 2017
by Jessica Kingsley Publishers
73 Collier Street
London N1 9BE, UK
and
400 Market Street, Suite 400
Philadelphia, PA 19106, USA

www.jkp.com

Copyright © Jessica Kingsley Publishers 2017
Foreword copyright © Paul Gilbert 2017

Library of Congress Cataloging in Publication Data
Title: Sharing compassion : fostering hope and resilience in clinical
    practice / edited by Sarah Parry.
Description: London ; Philadelphia : Jessica Kingsley Publishers, 2017.
Identifiers: LCCN 2017002396 (print) | LCCN 2017009708 (ebook) | ISBN
    9781785920707 (alk. paper) | ISBN 9781784503314 (ebook)
Subjects: LCSH: Psychotherapy. | Compassion. | Psychotherapist and patient.
Classification: LCC RC480.5 .S4444 2017 (print) | LCC RC480.5 (ebook) | DDC
    616.89/14--dc23

British Library Cataloguing in Publication Data
A CIP catalogue record for this book is available from the British Library

ISBN 978 1 78592 070 7
eISBN 978 1 78450 331 4

Printed and bound in the United States

Contents

Foreword

Professor Paul Gilbert

The last few years have seen increasing research and interest in the role of prosocial, helping, caring and compassionate behaviour on a range of physiological, psychological and social processes. There are now a number of different models of compassion that offer different insights into this important dynamic of human activity. We can trace the origins of compassion to reproductive strategies linked to caring for offspring and on into the value of mutual self-help. We can begin to identify some of the neurophysiological mechanisms that evolved to support prosocial behaviour (e.g. the myelinated parasympathetic system of the vagus nerve, the role of oxytocin and the frontal cortex) rather than pure competitive self-interest. All of this builds towards increasing our understanding of how we function at our best when we feel safe, caring and cared for. Neoliberal agendas, which support unregulated competitive self-interest, tribalism and defensiveness, are actually in the long run detrimental to our health, our relationships, organisations and societies.

While competitive motives have a place, unbalanced competitive societies breed social comparison and playing people off against each other. This in turn can be a source for self-criticism too rooted in the fear of rejection or not being good enough. The objectification of the self as object in the cogs of production. We feel the solution is simply to become better, a more efficient cog, even to the point of being perfect and then launch frustrative attacks on ourselves when we are imperfect. This dynamic is beautifully explored personally in the opening chapters. Also explored is the nature of compassion in different communities and cultures, and in particular the interplay between organisational processes and the giving and receiving of compassion, particularly, but not only, in healthcare settings.

So the science of compassion is increasingly robust, important and urgent. But there is another side to compassion that is related to lived experience and the narratives that we create and the insights we obtain through living and working with compassion. In this collection of chapters, you will find wonderful contributions to that side of thinking about compassion. In what follows is a series of personal reflections on how compassion has been both a challenge but also a journey into different dimensions of self and self in relationship. There are times when our deepest insights come not from laboratories or statistical tests but from realisations that arise from lived experience. This is a contribution to that journey and those insights.

Professor Paul Gilbert, PhD, FBPsS, OBE

Preface

SHARING STORIES AS A MEANS OF
EXPLORING EXPERIENCES

——————— Dr Sarah Parry ———————

*Senior Lecturer at Manchester Metropolitan
University, Clinical Psychologist*

Like many psychologists, my first introduction to research was based on a system of numbers, numerical analyses and transforming information (or *data*) into quantifiable representations that could be turned into tables and graphs. Sure enough, numbers have their place and much of the most influential research in healthcare uses extremely high volumes of data, which can tell us about important patterns and outcomes in healthcare services. However, although this research can tell us lots of important information about *what* happens and sometimes *when* changes occur, significant messages around *why* and *how* people have certain experiences can be lost.

Whilst undertaking one particular piece of research some years ago, I heard how extremely creative children with imaginary friends developed wonderfully rich stories based on a simple wordless storybook. I unquestioningly turned the stories into numbers, tables and graphs before asking my supervisor whether I could discuss the stories I had heard using the words of the children (qualitative research), rather than through numbers alone. After an uncomfortably long pause, his reply was: 'But what would that *mean?*' I understood this as a 'no', although his question stayed with me as I learnt new ways to explore and report the human experience and the ways in which we develop meaning around our experiences. A few years later, clinical psychology training introduced me to ways of doing research based on exploring the meaning people made of their experiences through formulation and qualitative research. It wasn't always an easy introduction, but it helped to make research mean more to me.

This qualitative and meaning-based approach helped me to not only enjoy research, but also meaningfully connect my clinical work and skills with research to get the best results. It has been my experience that many qualitative papers are extremely effective at communicating meaning through the voices of the people who take part in the research and the salient conclusions the author(s) draw from their analyses. For me personally, this was the way forward.

The temptation, perhaps particularly early on in our academic careers, is to cover up what we don't know with ambiguity, to thrust a sense of intellectualisation through our writing or to assume everyone knows more than us and so avoid being too explicit, all of which can often result in important messages being lost. Writing traps that I know I have certainly fallen into many times! In my personal journey, it was not until my doctoral studies that I had the experience of being permitted to focus on qualitative research exclusively. Prioritising the voices of the participants and exploring how people made sense of their experiences guided my research and furthered my interest in the utility of safe spaces for sharing stories and enhancing understanding of and compassion towards the self and others. As has been suggested by other mental health researchers, 'Understanding suffering is, after all, central to compassion' (Spandler and Stickley 2011, p.559).

As my research started to move into the realms of trying to understand how people healed from trauma and reconnect to themselves and others, I found new ways of working with their information to preserve the meaning of their experiences and perspectives. This could not have been done without the guidance and support of an enthusiastic, dedicated and nurturing clinical doctoral team at the University of Lancaster. The result has been life changing, not only because I now genuinely enjoy and look forward to the research elements of my job, but also because developing a means for understanding the complex and multi-layered experiences we have as humans connected to ourselves, each other, our past experiences and our future hopes and fears transcends across all aspects of life. It is within this context of accepting a position of 'not knowing', with the promise of exploration and the chance of understanding, that research and practice, art and science, listeners and storytellers can come together to share stories and shed light upon some of the most complex experiences we have.

> Story telling is about connecting to other people and helping people to see what you see.
>
> Michael Margolis (2016)

Within this book, my colleagues and I share our stories of practising compassion and reflect on how this influences our work and our experience of ourselves and professional identity, and how shared compassion in health and social care can nurture our capacity for hope and foster resilience.

Setting the language scene

If words are the 'heart of language' (Lewis 1993, p.89), we should consider some important words within this book and their meaning, before exploring the meaning-making processes of the contributors through their written narratives. Naturally, *compassion* is the first word and meaning we need to discuss. There are many ways of defining compassion in various contexts, although this book adopts the definition coined by the Compassionate Mind Foundation (2015): 'a sensitivity to suffering in self and others with a commitment to try to alleviate and prevent it'. As I have tried to learn more about compassion and understand how it protects and restores wellbeing, as someone who works closely with people experiencing distress, I return time and time again to the work and writings of Pema Chödrön (The Pema Chödrön Foundation 2017), as she so beautifully recognises the mutuality and dynamic nature of compassion in working practice:

> In cultivating compassion we draw from the wholeness of our experience – our suffering, our empathy, as well as our cruelty and terror. It has to be this way. Compassion is not a relationship between the healer and the wounded. It's a relationship between equals. Only when we know our own darkness well can we be present with the darkness of others. Compassion becomes real when we recognise our shared humanity. (The Pema Chödrön Foundation 2017)

The conclusion I often reach with colleagues and students in discussions around the possibility of cultivating and nurturing compassion is that there must be a shared willingness and trust within a pairing, small community or group of people in order for compassion to be present and accepted, which can encourage self-compassion to grow. Kristin Neff, a leading academic and international presence around self-compassion, has concluded that *self-compassion* requires 'three main elements: kindness, a sense of common humanity and mindfulness' (Neff and Germer 2013, p.1). The concept of self-compassion is particularly important for health and social care practitioners to implement due to the evidenced link between self-compassion and positive wellbeing (e.g. Barnard and Curry 2011; Trompetter, de Kleine and Bohlmeijer 2016).

The other two key concepts this book hopes to explore in relation to practising compassion are *hope* and *resilience*. The indisputable father of defining and explaining *hope* is C. R. Snyder, who identifies the process of hope as 'the perceived capability to derive pathways to desired goals, and motivate oneself via agency thinking to use those pathways' (2002, p.249). This pragmatic understanding of hope can be very powerful within our professions, as it helps us understand our role, thinking and actions in realising our goals and desires, rather than hope being a feeling passively experienced. Further, as I will explain, considering hope in this way connects hope, shared compassion and resilience as complementing processes. I became particularly interested in the link between compassion, hope and resilience as I extended my work with looked-after children to researching what helped young people ageing out of the care system (Parry and Weatherhead 2014). My practical work with young people had shown me so much about the important links between relationships, connection and one's capacity for hope and resilience. However, this research convinced me that when young people have at least one person they can rely on, all of their cognitive and emotional abilities are boosted. Through combining the stories of young people ageing out of care, it was clear that if a young person had someone whom they could trust, their ability to problem solve, dig deep, navigate a complex care system and manage difficulties that most people their age are never asked to face was enhanced. Although a rather generic definition, the American Psychological Association (2016) explains *resilience* as 'the process of adapting well in the face of adversity, trauma, tragedy, threats or significant sources of stress – such as family and relationship problems, serious health problems or workplace and financial stressors. It means "bouncing back" from difficult experiences.' It is the ability to 'bounce back' that is crucial to wellbeing, although it is the experience of having something to bounce back from, explicitly the experience of challenge itself, that offers the platform for developing an internal springboard and hope that new pathways for trying again can be found and followed through.

Within a framework of thinking about compassion, hope and resilience in these ways, there are several other key concepts and words we need to consider: *acceptance, accountability, empathy, empathic warmth* and *self-kindness*. To paraphrase Tara Brach (2017), *acceptance* is the process of recognising the truth of the moment in the moment with a courageous quality, the willingness of our heart to fully engage in being present – a state of body–mind – and how we can relate to the current reality, without evaluation, 'just as it is'. Therefore, acceptance can be seen as a willingness to feel emotions and a tolerance of emotions, to notice them without evaluation. Accepting emotions in this way can facilitate working through them to accept the reality, not the actions of others or ourselves, but our response to those actions in the moment. Although compassion, self-kindness and acceptance can often lead to connotations of 'letting oneself off the hook', 'self-indulgence' and 'lacking accountability', compassionate acceptance can enhance our capacity for struggle, so we actually become more accountable to our reactions and ways of responding to challenge. Accordingly, *accountability* is a huge part of practising compassion, perhaps especially in health and social care. As O'Donnell (2016) explains:

> compassionate accountability is a commitment to kind self-truth telling. It is the act of stepping up to the authorship of your life. It is the gentle re-establishment of faith bounded by principles that you protect just as much for yourself as you do for others. It is the courage to act heroically when the person to be rescued is you.

It is hard to imagine how authentic therapeutic alliances and collegial relationships could function without accountability, which is perhaps why relations between practitioners and politicians have become as strained as they have been in recent years.

Finally, we come to three terms that are often misconstrued or misused: *empathy, empathic warmth* and *self-kindness*. Empathy, often mistaken for sympathy, is a fundamental aspect of any meaningful relationship and the essence of how we can view an experience from the viewpoint of another. I refer to a quote from social worker, speaker and shame researcher Brené Brown (2012), who has also developed a fantastic video about empathy, the details of which are available in the 'further reading' section of this book:

> The most powerful tool of compassion, empathy is an emotional skill that allows us to respond to others in a meaningful, caring way. Empathy is the ability to understand what someone is experiencing and reflect that understanding back, not feeling it for them. If someone is feeling lonely, empathy doesn't require us to feel lonely, too, only to reach back into our own experience with loneliness so we can understand and connect.

The reason this is especially important for people in caring professions, as well as for people managing and overseeing people in caring professions, is because of the dynamic nature of empathy – we don't just do, we feel! To do what we do *well*, we don't just observe suffering, we reconnect with an experience of suffering and turn that into something usable for connection. However, after this, we must restore and attend to our own encounter with distress. Fully embraced and experienced empathy is different from empathic warmth. *Empathic warmth* can be defined as a non-judgemental warmth and a genuine desire to understand and supportively 'hold' the wellbeing of another or self. This could be seen as the 'top layer' of what we as helping professionals do. We are able to provide empathic warmth because of our ability to experience empathy safely and professionally. With these additional requirements on our emotional resources, it is all the more important to implement *self-kindness*: 'Self-kindness helps us take the perspective of an "other" toward ourselves. It lets in a breath of fresh air, so we see our pain from a different – more detached – vantage point' (Neff 2016). The ability to view suffering, strengths, virtues and qualities from the perspective of an 'other' can nurture self-kindness and offer much needed restoration to sometimes upsetting and depleting experiences. Although it is always an honour to bear witness to the struggles and striving of the people we work with, being fully engaged in suffering can take its toll. Recognising this and actively restoring ourselves afterwards is an essential part of the process of being an effective health and social care practitioner.

Taking shared humanity from under the shadows of the professional cloak: recognising, restoring and repairing oneself for care

Before we launch into the wonderfully honest and insightful stories from my generous colleagues, let us take some time to think about why the stories and messages in this book are useful and timely. I would like to start by saying that I love my job. I am immensely grateful to all of the individual people, groups, organisations and systems that helped me to train through a funded doctorate in clinical psychology – it is an enormous honour and privilege to have had the experience of training with people who align themselves with a profession that invests in supporting people to make their lives richer, healthier and happier. That said, working in health services can be very hard! In 2014, the Health Improvement Analytical Team within England's Department of Health released a factsheet of information titled: *Healthcare Sector Staff Wellbeing, Service Delivery and Health Outcomes*. Although the information contained in the report was not new news to many of us, for instance that practitioner wellbeing or burnout impacts service delivery and patient wellbeing, the language was a little surprising. One extract read:

The importance of compassion in health care has been reaffirmed by a number of government reviews including the Francis Review on the mid-Staffordshire NHS Foundation Trust (2013); the review into the commissioning of care and treatment at Winterbourne View care home in Bristol (2001); and the Keogh Review investigation into the care and treatment provided by 14 hospital trusts identified as having higher than average death rates. (p.4)

Compassion, it seemed, had been recognised as the missing component, not from individual practitioners but from the overarching management systems. As the Francis Report (Powell 2013) put it, the 'business of the system' was being prioritised over patients' needs. Amidst growing concern in England that neoliberal government policies and a target-driven culture were driving down staff wellbeing and outcomes, the British Psychological Society and New Savoy Partnership took action. During 2014 and 2015, a survey of over 1300 psychological practitioners was conducted, with shocking results. The survey reported that almost half of those who responded reported depression and feelings of failure, 70 per cent said they found their job stressful and experiences of bullying and harassment had more than doubled. Although there are many professions where you may expect to find such figures, psychological practitioners have historically reported high work satisfaction rates and, most importantly, require wellbeing to do their work effectively. The survey results led to a *Charter for Psychological Staff Wellbeing and Resilience* (British Psychological Society and New Savoy Partnership 2015) and a series of initiatives to get things back on track. However, in the current political and economic climate, change may be slow and this picture of burnout and work stressors negatively influencing staff wellbeing seems to be a recurring problem across the health professions (Bolier *et al.* 2014).

In such working environments, hope can be understood as both a catalyst and preserving factor of recovery (Schrank, Stanghellini and Slade 2008; Spandler and Stickley 2011). As helping professionals, and perhaps as people who care for family members and friends outside of work too, we all need to recover and recharge ourselves at points. Healing and restoring ourselves following particular challenges is a key part of practising safely and healthily in our roles. In their review of the importance of hope and compassion within mental health services, social worker Spandler and mental health nurse and counsellor Stickley (2011) discuss how it is frequently recommended that mental health practitioners promote a sense of hope in others, although little is really understood about how hope can be nurtured within services systemically, which is perhaps why it is so noticeably absent from written mental health policies and staff support strategies. In other work connecting hope and compassion, which importantly involved the voices of young people who faced multiple and concurrent socioemotional and economic challenges, the young people explained that attuned social workers facilitated inspiring hope through experiencing compassion (Guthrie et al. 2014, p.131). The young people explained that when compassion underpinned the relationship with their social worker, they were able to feel a connection and, subsequently, hopefulness.

As aforementioned, this book discusses hope as conceptualised and defined by C.R. Snyder, whose Hope Theory proposes that our goals provide *targets* for hopeful thinking (Snyder 2002), which operationalise as two processes: *pathways,* the planning process to achieve goals, and the *agency* with which a person perceives their abilities to follow their pathways to the goals. Together, these processes lead to a person achieving their goals and realising their hope, nurturing further hopefulness. Snyder (2000) also explains how hope supports resilience, as a person can use their sense of agency to overcome barriers, fostering a sense of determination towards challenge and adversity. A few years ago, I stumbled across an article that both challenged and enriched my understanding of what resilience is and how it might work. Whilst considering the role of hope in healing from adversity, the review article by Harvey and Delfabbro (2004) came along at just the right time for me to connect a few dots together in terms of my own experiences and noticings in practice with young people. As Harvey and Delfabbro discuss their developing psychological framework for understanding resilience across cultural and social boundaries, they crucially highlight the importance of circularity within the framework, in that factors that seem to cultivate resilience are also nurtured by resilience. For example, effective problem solving or the ability to recognise one's limitations and seek support can be both causes and outcomes of resilience. Also, Harvey and Delfabbro state that people need to have faced challenging experiences in order to experience resilience, i.e. to have something to bounce back from and get a better sense of their *agency* and ability to manage adversity, which in turn may give the person more or less optimism about facing hardship at another time. In these ways, hope and resilience are deeply connected bi-directional processes that influence one another. The missing piece of the puzzle, which I didn't consider until a few years later, was the role of shared compassion as the environment around hope and resilience, which could either give their flames room to breathe or, if absent, stifle them.

Just as hope requires goal-orientated behaviour and resilience often requires direct personal experience of struggle, the young people in the study of Guthrie *et al.* described compassion as 'action-oriented' in response to a witnessed need or distress. This response could come in a number of forms, including 'listening, acceptance, affectionate outreach, insight, and/or resources (e.g. money, food, a seat on a bus)' and that 'receiving compassion instilled hope in the cared-for person' (2014, p.133). The young people suggested that through modelling compassion and encouraging them to find pathways to desired resolutions and futures, the social workers were nurturing their own resilience. In other work, Hernández, Gangsei and Engstrom (2007) undertook a thorough analysis of interviews with psychotherapists to explore the opposite of *vicarious trauma* (simply, the vicarious experience of another's trauma), which they called *vicarious resilience*, the ability to 'reframe negative events' and to have their 'coping skills enhanced' though witnessing the resilience of their clients during trauma work (p.240). Within the hope and resilience literature, the recurring finding is that all of us need at least one reliable person to show and demonstrate kindness and compassion in order for hope and resilience to ignite and take flame (Harvey and Delfabbro 2004; Parry and Weatherhead 2014). As beautifully stated by Guthrie *et al.*, 'hope is ignited by receiving compassion' (2014, p.138), and perhaps kept aflame through the cyclical experiences of sharing compassion with another and practising strategies, finding pathways and advancing agency, demonstrating one's own abilities in the face of adversity and feeding a sense of competency. For this reason, health and social care practitioners have many of the resources necessary to keep their compassionate, hopeful and resilient flames alive if the working environments around them provide suitable support, supervision and a space for reflection to tell their stories.

Recently, Israeli social worker and academic Orit Nuttman-Shwartz has pulled many experiential personal and professional threads together through her work looking at the personal impact of therapeutic work, often in settings where trauma has been a shared experience, such as during national conflicts. She discusses the many positive side effects of working with people healing from trauma, including 'compassion satisfaction (Figley 2002), vicarious PTG [posttraumatic growth] (VPTG; Arnold, *et al.* 2005), adversarial growth (Linley, Jospeh, and Loumidis 2005), and, most recently, vicarious resilience (Hernández, Gangsei and Engstrom 2007)' (2016, p.466). Perhaps most interestingly, Nuttman-Shwartz explicitly discusses the mutual process of growing resilience that therapists can experience in trauma work as a result of witnessing the strength of the human spirit and how clients cope with extreme stress. Crucially, Nuttman-Shwartz discusses the cyclical and dynamic nature of resilience as the client demonstrates resilience, which is witnessed by the therapist, who then incorporates these novel ways of coping into intervention design, resulting in effective strategies for both client and therapist in the face of adversity. Other theorists and practitioners have noticed similar processes, through which embracing struggles whilst relating positively to oneself, which can happen independently of relating positively to failings or mistakes, can facilitate 'happiness, optimism, wisdom, curiosity and exploration, personal initiative, and emotional intelligence... interpersonal functioning...perspective taking and forgiveness' (Neff and Germer 2013, p.3) through practising self-compassion. As practitioners, many of us are lucky enough to have a safe space for exploring these processes through supervision, although we can also nurture such space for safe struggle and reflection through writing reflective narratives about our experiences, developing peer support groups and cultivating working environments to share struggle and compassion.

A personal and professional disclaimer...

When this book initially started out, it was to be a clinical handbook for practitioners interested in the restorative power of shared compassion in their practice. However, as the chapters started to come through, it was clear that this book was going to be a collection of bravely written, whole-self, personal and professional accounts. Therefore, it seemed only right to be clear about my own lived experiences with sharing compassion too...

A bumpy and ongoing road to self-kindness and sharing compassion

As practitioners, we are all aware of the many health benefits of compassion and hope for our clients and patients in terms of physical health, emotional wellbeing and healing (Decety and Fotopoulou 2015; Hamilton 2010; Spandler and Stickley 2011). However, most training programmes for practitioners spend much less time, if any, exploring the role of self-compassion and shared compassion for practitioners. When considered objectively, this is strange, as empirical research (e.g. Fernando and Consedine 2014; Firth-Cozens and Cornwell 2009) and personal anecdotes (see the Healthcare Network 2016) tell us time and again that working in stressful and unsupported environments directly threatens compassion. Preoccupations with financial savings, the stress of working with complex illnesses and a culture of blame and scapegoating will naturally put anyone's ability for compassion under attack. Is it perhaps that people in caring professions are expected to be immune from these pressures? Are we expected to be so driven by our need to care for others that we won't notice these external attacks to our own wellbeing?

I have worked in some fairly intense environments (British understatement) and have, at least on some level, always understood the need for and value of self-care – that is looking after one's own needs. However, for many years, I think I looked after my own needs just enough and when convenient, in order to get on with whatever job was in hand. It wasn't until I began doctoral work and study with two young children that I realised I might (British understatement translation – 'absolutely must or face certain breakdown') need to develop my skills in this area. I looked around me and wondered how some people managed to disentangle themselves from work when they got home, genuinely care about the people they supported through their work and then seamlessly, accountably and compassionately leave work at work for the day to be fully attentive with their families. This was an incredible and somewhat mythical skill to me.

As I considered the internal and external influences upon how I approached my work, I began to question where some of my needs to succeed, excel and be seen to be coping came from. During the 1980s and 1990s, my grandad did a lot of research around our family tree and the lives of our ancestors. As a child and teen, I would hear the newly discovered family stories and saw how these stories seemed to give new roots to the family as a whole. I loved hearing about the fiery Celts from Glencoe and the three sisters from the Victorian era who worked their way from the orphanage to become London-based property proprietors. Closer to home, I imagined the adventurous spirit of my maternal grandmother who had lived in Canada for a while and worked in the Women's Auxiliary Air Force during World War II. I also heard how my paternal grandparents had fallen in love as teenagers and healed together from the traumas of war to build a new life. I looked back and realised that the running theme through the stories I had heard was striving. There must have been many people who lived quiet lives, maybe moved to a new area or worked in a particular job, although their stories had been lost to time. Going forwards, success and overcoming challenges were the dominant family and individual themes left.

When I was 18 years old, I was lucky enough to be invited to work as a volunteer in a day centre in Romania that aimed to support looked-after children who lived in the local orphanages. My first visit was transformational for me, as I witnessed extreme hardship and inspirational resilience from the young people themselves, staff and volunteers. Within six months of my first trip to Romania, motivated by a search for purpose and meaning, I was running a successful and hectic arm of the organisation, which I had developed with the help and support of some amazing people – particularly a specialist nurse called Jayne Harris who remains one of the most inspiring people I have ever known. Our work, largely involving enthusiastic students and I, facilitated volunteers to help with basic psychosocial interventions to enhance the social and communicative skills of the young people we aimed to support in the day centre and surrounding orphanages. Over the next two years, our volunteer network grew extremely quickly and we hosted over a hundred volunteers a year, found new sponsors and partners, and raised fairly large sums of money for sustainable long-term projects. We also worked with various health and social care professionals to tailor evidence-based therapeutic models and approaches in an attempt to meet the unique needs of the young people we worked with across a growing number of locations. It was exciting, hugely rewarding, often fun and yet also completely overwhelming and exhausting.

One morning in Romania, I was feeling particularly overwhelmed as we reached yet another financial hurdle on the road to establishing a permanent home for some of the children who we hoped to rehome from their orphanage, which was being shut down. I felt utterly depleted and unqualified for the work I was doing, and was full of anxiety for what lay ahead (lacking in both hopeful pathways and agency). Covered in mosquito bites, exhausted from what seemed like constant travelling and juggling a full-time degree course and work, my eyes dry with lack of sleep and the burning July heat, I was truly questioning whether I was doing the right thing. I could think of so many people better placed and qualified to carry things forward. Feeling low and washed out, I sat under a tree for some shade with one of the young girls I had gotten to know well; we will call her Ana. Ana didn't communicate with words but, as is often the case, knew exactly how to get her point across. As we played with some cups and water under the tree, she gave me all sorts of cues to be a bit more engaged. However, on this particular morning, I was really struggling to play enthusiastically. The game paused, and I remember looking at Ana pouring all the water from the cups onto the grass with one hand and sucking her thumb, as she often did, with the other. Ana then turned to me and put her other thumb up to my face and gestured while half smiling. It dawned on me that, seeing I was upset about something, Ana had perhaps thought about what made her feel better and possibly wondered if her approach to self-soothing might help me too.

In that moment, I forgot all about my aches, pains, itchy bites and tiredness, instead only feeling somehow reconnected, restored and hopeful again. I didn't even really have the words for my change in mood or perception at the time, but as I have become more aware of shared compassion over the years, I see that experience under the tree with Ana as my first clear introduction to the restorative power of shared compassion. I saw then that Ana and I were just two people, born to very different circumstances, just going along doing the best we could. From then on, my whole approach to our work in Romania changed. We were no longer a group of volunteers working to support children who we thought should have been getting better care from the staff teams – we were all, collectively, just people doing the best we could. This new perspective helped me see and imagine what it must have been like for the residential staff in those orphanages, with so few resources, long shifts and no real control over the hard environments they worked in. Our working relationships changed and over the next few years, our work increased in focus and momentum as we worked more closely with the care staff in Romania and elsewhere: sharing stories, meals and even an international skills exchange one year. There was a new sense of togetherness and hopefulness, which facilitated many other positive steps over the next few years. This framework of sharing experiences and abandoning hierarchies has influenced how I think and work ever since. Compassion, albeit in a very unpolished and undefined way, became my new framework for trying to understanding many situations – while things were going fairly well at least.

However, skip forward a few years past a Master's degree, postgraduate jobs in community mental healthcare, joyfully becoming a mother to my son and daughter and a trainee clinical psychologist, things were not going so well. A framework of striving and juggling competing demands had once again overtaken a framework for living with compassion and the warm calmness that had beautifully surrounded my world as a new mother. Driven by a force of not feeling *good enough* and as sleep deprivation continued to take its toll on my ability to juggle all the balls I had in the air, it dawned on me that I had striven too far too quickly and was in the process of falling over. For the first 18 months of my doctoral studies, I staggered through a fog of exhaustion, experiencing all sorts of unusual things such as hair loss, losing feeling in my hands and feet and feeling incredibly detached at times. Having never fully accepted before that I couldn't cover all the bases I had created for myself all the time, and succumbing to the practical necessities that accompany having to hold down a job and be a full-time mother as well, I carried on pushing through, ignoring the recurring colds and knowing I was not performing at my best.

In this setting, my critical-self thrived, highlighting all of my failings, shortcomings and disappointments. In a working environment where everyone was academically and practically talented, my struggles were very clear. My clinical practice provided me with opportunities to practise compassion with the people I worked with. However, I knew something very important was missing and that I needed to address it. Although I was attending to my needs in some ways, spending as much time as I could with my children, family and friends, exercising and eating well, I still wasn't quite meeting my emotional needs. In her most recent book, *Rising Strong*, Brené Brown suggests, 'Giving doesn't exist without giving and receiving. We need to give and we need to need. This is true at work and at home' (2015, p.182). In my merged roles as 'carer' at home and at work, I struggled enormously to give myself permission to need, to take time, to work as hard as I knew I needed to in order to learn, to prioritise my learning and need to study. In a vacuous space of 'never enough', I struggled to understand the compassion and patience shown to me by fellow colleagues. In particular, I couldn't quite understand the patience of my line manager, the inspirationally kind and steady Dr Anna Daiches. With my two children being new to childcare and with my own immune system struggling with the various bugs they brought home, I was off work a lot in the first few months, nursing either my children or myself, which gave my self-critic all the fuel it needed to find further reasons as to why I had bitten off more than I could chew. I became increasingly anxious that I would not make it through my training contract, either failing outright or being asked to leave. Consequently, with personal resources lacking, I turned to a good friend.

In life, many of us are lucky enough to meet many potential friends and, more luckily still, some of them stick with us and stay firm friends through the years. My friends have always been an assorted, disparate bunch: old friends from my teens, some fellow party girls, likeminded parents, some working companions and some tranquil jewels. Then, there are the lemon-juice friends – the ones who make you squint and your eyes water with their citric clarity that can cut through all sorts of crap! I have two lemon-juice friends, whose judgement and perspective are often delivered during crucial times. During one such conversation with a lemon-juice friend, also called Sarah, I was rambling about my increasing insecurities and worries about not being able to keep up with my colleagues and concerns that I was making too many compromises in my parenting. It went something like this:

Me: I just can't shake off the worry that I'm not doing enough and what I do do isn't good enough anyway...they'll think I'm too unreliable and unavailable to do the job properly...they can't really be as understanding as they're saying...I mean...I...

Sarah: You'd have fired your ass by now!

Me: Whaa...?

Sarah: You wouldn't have hired you in the first place, would you! [This was a rhetorical question.]

Me: [Annoyed look, followed by nodding.]

Difficult as it was to hear and accept, it was spot on. In my line manager's shoes, I would have calmly and politely pointed out that this 'perhaps wasn't the best time' and asked whether this was "a realistic undertaking".' My doubtful critic, lacking in the ability to nurture hope, would have triumphed and very nearly did. Once again, I saw how compassion was directly linked to hope and resilience, thankfully just in time to not let my internal self-critic take the reins. In my role as a senior lecturer now, I try as much as possible to walk in Anna's shoes, creating a compassionate space to hold hopeful uncertainty for what people may be able to achieve with the right support.

At a similar time, I had started to receive academic supervision from someone known for her keen eye for error, critical appraisal and unflinchingly honest feedback. However, to my surprise, rather than fuelling my self-critic, faced with this external critic, my self-critic seemed to calm down. As though my self-critic knew the critical angle was covered, it became easier to embrace self-kindness and to soothe. This was a particular revelation for me, as my self-critic was very much in control when it came to academic success – she was really good at filtering out everything apart from the task in hand and driving the task home.

However, my self-critic's way of working was neither practical nor sustainable as an adult with a hectic schedule and competing demands. Therefore, change was necessary and seemed to be happening in a supervisory relationship where I did not need to hold the critical space. With the needs of my self-critic seemingly met, there was space to learn to self-soothe, to consider the importance of 'good enough' and to create new pathways towards my hoped-for targets. Encouraged by paced and measured hard work over time, with space for reflection and learning rather than the boom-and-bust patterns that were so familiar, my hopeful agency began to return. Borrowing further hope from friends and colleagues seemed to provide the necessary agency with which to pursue these new hopeful pathways to a successful end.

Within this newfound space for reflection and contemplation, I looked around me and saw how many people in the healthcare settings where I was working as a trainee clinical psychologist also seemed to also struggle with finding a balance that enabled a sense of equilibrium, wellbeing and the ability to let go of the personal critical scrutiny evaluating what is 'good enough'. Without fully realising it, I had always had a sense of 'why do something good enough when you can do it better?', which is all well and good when the resources are available to draw upon, but a dangerous way of being when resources are limited. I began talking to colleagues who seemed to find and preserve this balance well. I was desperate to know what their secret was – how they did it, how they kept all the balls in the air and recovered when one dropped.

It turned out that a particular type of acceptance was crucial – an accepting kindness that was not based around success or failure but just a way of being and trying one's best. As I started talking to friends and colleagues, it dawned on me how many of the people I knew who found this difficult to understand, let alone take on board, myself included, worked in health and social care and often adopted a 'caring role' in other settings too. Why can caring people find self-kindness so difficult? I also started to see that those who could internalise kindness tended to be less adversely influenced by some of the challenges we face in the healthcare system.

I had worked in health and social care across various organisations throughout the recession that firmly took hold in the UK 2009 and had witnessed the panic, cuts, restructures and shared concern for the future of services and staff. From 2011, when I joined the National Health Service (NHS) as a trainee clinical psychologist, it was clear that challenge, change and uncertainty were going to be permanent pillars of working life for the foreseeable future. Since then, we have seen a swift movement towards the privatisation of the NHS and the enormous changes that movement has meant for patients and staff.

In her recent article reviewing the need for compassionate leadership in healthcare, de Zulueta, a general practitioner and therapist, discusses concerns that healthcare provisions in many countries are at risk of losing their 'moral compass' and that social, political, technological and financial influences are significantly impacting the nature of healthcare provisions (2015, p.1). She also discusses how the confusion in perception between compassion and emotional empathy is perhaps at the root of why some practitioners consider compassion in the same category as over-identification, collusion and unprofessionalism. Within this book, I and the other authors will discuss what compassion is and is not, so as to highlight the crucial role for compassion for health and social care practitioners and indeed anyone who cares for another.

Prior to doctoral training, I had become all too familiar with the concepts of compassion fatigue (Figley 1995), burnout and vicarious trauma (Pearlman and Saakvirne 1995) through my work overseas, which was largely emotionally unsupported, as is much voluntary humanitarian work. Being young and inexperienced myself, I assumed it was normal and expected to have the odd nightmare about some of the suffering we bore witness to or to feel a little numb sometimes towards the constant challenges we were trying to alleviate in a small way. In relation to compassion fatigue specifically, Kapoulitsas and Corcoran discuss how helping professionals can be particularly likely to have the experience due to the interplay between their 'capacity to demonstrate empathy, coupled with exposure to challenging situations including but not limited to threats to personal safety, unpredictability and exposure to narratives of distress' (2015, p.98). Although their study is rooted in social work, I am sure many of us from a range of health and social care professions can strongly relate to this cocktail of experiences. It was not until I started looking for the shared humanity and shared struggles, thanks to Ana, that compassionate growth led the way to curiosity, shared understanding and appreciating the levels of stress that we were all experiencing. I knew, at some level, that there was something hugely restorative about embracing the shared struggle and appreciating the ways in which we were all getting through, doing the best we could. Nevertheless, with little time and space for reflection, and little knowledge of how to reflexively reflect upon these experiences, looking back, a lot of learning opportunities were probably lost. Indeed, a key finding from Kapoulitsas and Corcoran's study around compassion fatigue for social workers was that a 'supportive work environment and positive supervision played a pivotal role in shaping what accounted for resilience' and the opportunity for the practitioner to 'speak openly about their experiences in a safe environment' was invaluable to wellbeing (2015, p.98).

During doctoral training, we had weekly supervision, which at first felt like a luxury and an opportunity to check out whether I was mechanistically on track in terms of 'doing' the work. My first two supervisors quickly and seamlessly created a safe space for me to talk openly, without worry of 'getting it wrong', through which I could think around and behind experiences and consider the experiences as a whole for learning. On one occasion when I was feeling a little stuck and bogged down in the detail of a piece of therapeutic work, my supervisor asked me: 'What are you learning about yourself in this?' It was such a helpful question and a question I continue to ask myself in a range of forms whenever I am starting to feel stuck. In this particular instance, I had been wondering what to say, as I had been doing some work with a middle-aged man who had experienced a number of losses, which had a profound impact upon his relationships with those he loved and his sense of self. There had been many times in supervision previously when I had talked about the difficulties he was facing and the helplessness I felt at times in the face of such loss and sadness.

However, when faced with the question about what I was learning about myself from the experience, I was able to access some of the experiences that, at times, I felt uncomfortable discussing. I explained that I was surprised about the impact the work was having on me and how I was vicariously experiencing hope and pride as my client continued to make small changes to enhance his quality of life. As I came to the end of that particular placement in a community mental health team, I became increasingly aware of a sense of loss. A loss of something I had not seen as much in my work with children and young people – the power of seeing people take steps towards improving their lives and the honour of being with them for a part of that journey. I love working with children: I love their playfulness and hopefulness and knowing that time is on their side. However, children often have limited power and control over certain aspects of their lives, which makes them particularly vulnerable, and they are without the practical independence or experience to make certain changes and decisions, which is why we tend to work much more systemically in children's services. Working with adults in the community mental health team was my first experience of working largely one-to-one with clients and witnessing the power of autonomy combined with a conviction to enhance one's own wellbeing.

I wanted to learn more about how powerful processes such as borrowing hope, vicarious resilience and shared compassion could support self-kindness for practitioners, to help cope with working in an increasingly challenging environment in an already highly emotive job. I wanted to slow down the processes involved and see how self-kindness and shared compassion worked in practice for other health and social care professionals. The opportunity of developing this book gave me a chance to ask people with direct experience of these processes to share their stories. This enhances our understanding of how sharing compassion with the people we work with and ourselves can help restore and promote resilience and hope, which is essential in our line of work.

Throughout this book, practitioners have shared their honest stories and reflections around how sharing compassion can be powerful and difficult in practice, with many considering the contexts and cultures in which their self-critic thrived and self-kindness struggled to survive. However, through engaging with these complex processes and exploring the experiences that occur within us (intrapersonal), between us (interpersonal) and around us, we can start to see the integral value of shared compassion. Sharing compassion with our colleagues and clients is often what can make the important difference to healing, wellbeing, hope and resilience.

References

American Psychological Association (2016). *The Road to Resilience*. Available at www.apa.org/helpcenter/road-resilience.aspx, accessed on 21 February 2017.

Barnard, L. K. and Curry, J. F. (2011). Self-compassion: Conceptualizations, correlates, and interventions. *Review of General Psychology, 15*(4), 289–303.

Bolier, L., Ketelaar, S. M., Nieuwenhuijsen, K., Smeets, O., Gartner, F. R., and Sluiter, J. K. (2014). Workplace mental health promotion online to enhance well-being of nurses and allied health professionals: A cluster-randomized controlled trial. *Internet Interventions, 1*(4), 196–204.

Brach, T. (2017) *The Power of Radical Acceptance: Healing Trauma through the Integration of Buddhist Meditation and Psychotherapy*. Available at www.tarabrach.com/articles-interviews/trauma, accessed on 21 February 2017.

British Psychological Society and New Savoy Partnership (2015). *Charter for Psychological Wellbeing and Resilience*. Available at www.bps.org.uk/system/files/Public%20files/Comms-media/press_release_and_charter.pdf, accessed on 21 February 2017.

Brown, B. (2015). *Rising Strong: The Reckoning. The Rumble. The Revolution*. New York: Spiegel and Grau.

Brown, B. (2012). *Listening to Shame* [TED talk]. Available at www.ted.com/talks/brene_brown_listening_to_shame, accessed on 21 February 2017.

Compassionate Mind Foundation (2015). *About Us*. Available at http://compassionatemind.co.uk/about-us, accessed on 21 February 2017.

Decety, J. and Fotopoulou, A. (2015). Why empathy has a beneficial impact on others in medicine: Unifying theories. *Frontiers in Behavioral Neuroscience, 8*, 1–11.

Department of Health (2014). *A Compendium of Factsheets: Wellbeing Across the Lifecourse. Healthcare Sector Staff Wellbeing, Service Delivery and Health Outcomes*. Available at www.gov.uk/government/uploads/system/uploads/attachment_data/file/277591/Staff_wellbeing__service_delivery_and_health_outcomes.pdf, accessed on 21 February 2017.

Fernando, A. T. and Considine, N. S. (2014). Development and initial psychometric properties of the barriers to physician compassion questionnaire. *Postgraduate Medical Journal, 90*(1065), 388.

Figley, C. R. (1995). *Compassion Fatigue: Coping with Secondary Traumatic Stress Disorder in Those Who Treat the Traumatized*. Abingdon: Psychology Press.

Firth-Cozens, J. and Cornwell, J. (2009). *Enabling Compassionate Care in Acute Hospital Settings*. London: King's Fund. Available at www.kingsfund.org.uk/sites/files/kf/field/field_publication_file/poc-enabling-compassionate-care-hospital-settings-apr09.pdf, accessed on 21 February 2017.

Guthrie, D. D., Ellison, V. S., Sami, K. and McCrea, K. T. (2014). Clients' hope arises from social workers' compassion: African American youths' perspectives on surmounting the obstacles of disadvantage. *Families in Society, 95*(2), 131–139.

Hamilton, D. R. (2010). *Why Kindness is Good for You*. London: Hay House.

Harvey, J. and Delfabbro, P. (2004). Psychological resilience in disadvantaged youth: A critical overview. *Australian Psychologist, 39*(1), 3–13.

Healthcare Network (2016). By the end of my first year as a doctor, I was ready to kill myself. *The Guardian*, 5 January 2016. Available at www.theguardian.com/healthcare-network/views-from-the-nhs-frontline/2016/jan/05/doctor-suicide-hospital-nhs, accessed on 21 February 2017.

Hernández, P., Gangsei, D. and Engstrom, D. (2007). Vicarious resilience: A new concept in work with those who survive trauma. *Family Process, 46*(2), 229–241.

Kapoulitsas, M. and Corcoran, T. (2015). Compassion fatigue and resilience: A qualitative analysis of social work practice. *Qualitative Social Work, 14*(1), 86–101.

Lewis, M. (1993). *The Lexical Approach: The State of ELT and a Way Forward*. Hove: Global ELT, Christopher Wenger.

Margolis, M. (2016). *Get Storied*. Available at: www.getstoried.com/3-simple-ways-start-story, accessed on 21 February 2017.

Neff, K. (2016). Don't Fall into the Self-Esteem Trap: Try a Little Self-Kindness. *Mindful*. https://www.mindful.org/dont-fall-into-the-self-esteem-trap-try-a-little-self-kindness/?utm_content=buffera26f9&utm_medium=social&utm_source=facebook.com&utm_campaign=buffer, accessed on 13 June 2017.

Neff, K. D. and Germer, C. K. (2013). A pilot study and randomized controlled trial of the mindful Self-Compassion program. *Journal of Clinical Psychology, 69*(1), 28–44.

Nuttman-Shwartz, O. (2016). Research in a shared traumatic reality: Researchers in a disaster context. *Journal of Loss and Trauma: International Perspectives on Stress and Coping, 21*(3), 179–191.

O'Donnell, L. (2016). *Compassionate Accountability*. Available at: www.mindingmatters.com/wp-content/uploads/2016/05/COMPASSIONATE-ACCOUNTABILITY-ODONNELL2016.pdf, accessed on 21 February 2017.

Parry, S. and Weatherhead, S. (2014). A critical review of qualitative research into the experiences of young adults leaving foster care service. *Journal of Children's Services. 9*(4), 263–279.

Pearlman, L. A. and Saakvirne, K. W. (1995). *Trauma and the Therapist: Countertransference and Vicarious Traumatization in Psychotherapy with Incest Survivors (A Norton professional book)*. New York: W. W. Norton.

The Pema Chödrön Foundation (2017). *Articles*. Available at http://pemachodronfoundation.org/articles, accessed on 21 February 2017.

Powell, T. (2013). *The Francis Report (Report of the Mid-Staffordshire NHS Foundation Trust Public Inquiry) and the Government's Response*. Available at http://researchbriefings.files.parliament.uk/documents/SN06690/SN06690.pdf, accessed on 5 April 2017.

Schrank, B., Stanghellini, G. and Slade, M. (2008). Hope in psychiatry: A review of the literature. *Acta Psychiatrica Scandinavica, 118*(6), 421–433.

Spandler, H. and Stickley, T. (2011). No hope without compassion: The importance of compassion in recovery-focused mental health services. *Journal of Mental Health, 20*(6), 555–566.

Snyder, C. R. (2002). Hope theory: Rainbows of the mind. *Psychological Inquiry, 13*(4), 249–275.

Snyder, C. R. (2000). *Handbook of Hope Theory, Measures and Applications.* San Diego, CA: Academic Press.

Trompetter, H. R., de Kleine, E. and Bohlmeijer, E. T. (2016). Why does positive mental health buffer against psychopathology? An exploratory study on self-compassion as a resilience mechanism and adaptive emotion regulation strategy. *Cognitive Therapy and Research*, 41(3), 459.

de Zulueta, P. (2015). Developing compassionate leadership in health care: An integrative review. *Journal of Healthcare Leadership, 2016*(8), 1–10.

PART ONE

Bringing Compassion into Life and Practice

Although prioritising the needs of others can fulfil our desire to 'rescue', this is typically done at the expense of attending to our own wellbeing. Of course, whilst this may result in us neglecting some of our needs, the very act of prioritising another may be fulfilling other needs we have. This can make it difficult to notice and adjust these patterns in order to attend to ourselves appropriately. For self-compassion to work, this is a fairly fundamental adjustment to make.

Hannah Wilson and Ciara Joyce

1

Modelling Imperfection and Developing the Imperfect Self

REFLECTIONS ON THE PROCESS OF APPLYING SELF-COMPASSION

————————— Dr Hannah Wilson —————————

Clinical Psychologist and Ciara Joyce, Trainee Clinical Psychologist

As two clinical psychologists, early in their careers, the authors of this chapter reflect on their understanding of self-compassion and the merits of its practice. They acknowledge that their conceptualisation of self-compassion has not been static, but rather is a process that continues to unfold. They describe how this process has often been guided by thinking about what self-compassion is not, and how difficult it can be to practise, especially in stressful or pressured contexts. Having shared a similar path into their careers, both authors reflected on the perfectionist tendencies that drove them to achieve but that also marred the sense of satisfaction that could be gained from accomplishments. Throughout their time working together, and with like-minded colleagues, they began to understand the value of embracing their imperfections. This chapter chronicles some of the processes they underwent in making such realisations and some of the challenges they faced in attempting to practise in more self-compassionate ways. They also introduce their concept of the 'imperfect-self' as a new influence on their professional and personal development.

Introduction

The authors of this chapter are both clinical psychologists: one of us newly qualified (Hannah) and the other currently completing training

(Ciara). We first met in 2015 whilst working together in an adult mental health service. Our shared interest around compassion began in an obvious way when we co-facilitated a Compassion Focused Therapy (CFT; Gilbert 2010) group, which was our first experience of applying this particular therapeutic model. This group was run as a weekly therapeutic group over a six-month period, in a specialist adult mental health service.

As we debriefed and reflected on the group, we discovered a mutual curiosity around the concept of compassion: what it looks like, where it comes from and how it can be realised both personally and professionally. Through some of these discussions, we recognised that compassion for others had long been part of our value bases. We shared a keen interest in, and openness to learning about, the wellbeing of others (often in the absence of attending to our own!). We hypothesised about why and how this had developed, noticing common experiences such as being raised as only children, having a passion for travel, seeing new cultures and applying new learning. In connecting to each other's stories and experiences, we noted a disparity between our ability to show compassion for others as opposed to ourselves. This is something that we've continued to invest in and develop (cue long discussions over several glasses of red wine).

Compassion is generally defined as 'a deep sympathy and sorrow in the face of suffering, be it our own or that of someone else, together with a motivation or commitment to alleviate distress' (Welford 2012, p.65). As this suggests, compassion can flow in various directions, including self-to-self, other-to-self, and self-to-other. For the purposes of this chapter, we are going to focus on self-compassion; that is, the capacity to connect to ourselves with love and kindness and to nurture a self-acceptance without criticism or judgement.

When the opportunity to write a chapter for this book arose, we felt excited at the idea of sharing some of our reflections. After much deliberation (less wine, more tea), we realised that the 'penny-drop' moment for us had been in accepting that we were imperfect, that this was okay and that it was important to model both that acceptance and that imperfection for our clients and each other.

We acknowledge that our experiences and perspectives will not necessarily be shared by everyone, but we hope that they can contribute to the ongoing development of compassionate practice. In this chapter, we will first consider our understanding of self-compassion and how this developed in response to the high demands we placed on ourselves, and the challenges of clinical practice. We will then consider some of the potential barriers to practising self-compassion that we have witnessed, before thinking about ways to manage these. Finally, we will reflect on the importance of acknowledging and embracing our imperfect selves.

Self-compassion

When we were facilitating the CFT group, we had the good fortune of working with a colleague who, in her own words, 'modelled imperfection'. This was originally a tongue-in-cheek comment we would employ when we perceived we had been less than 'good enough' (i.e. perfect!) in preparing for the group…recalling the content of homework last week… or remembering to buy the milk. However, what began as a flippant comment became a mantra that got us through the group and our jobs, and has accompanied our personal development ever since. We noticed how it gave us permission to be imperfect, which in turn helped us feel more relaxed and at ease with ourselves. We were surprised at the level of relief we experienced in response to this. When we were being more 'real' (less superhuman), we noticed group members responding positively to this and sharing more of themselves. As the group progressed, the sense of 'us and them' (facilitators and group members) diminished and we felt we were part of a shared learning process.

Our learning from these experiences culminated in the understanding that we could not foster compassion in others without attending to our own relationship with it. As we started to engage in self-compassionate practices, we noticed an internal expectation that we would be 'good' at this, as therapists and reflective practitioners. In reality, it was difficult, challenging and unpleasant at times! We became more aware of our assumption that self-compassion had an on/off button that we, as clinicians, would be able to locate easily (if anyone has indeed located this button, do let us know). Needless to say, this left us feeling vulnerable and exposed yet again as less-than-perfect.

As soon as we named this assumption, we acknowledged both its understandable origin and total lack of foundation. We are first and foremost people, not clinicians, with all of the flaws, worries and insecurities that this brings. The process of engaging with self-compassion involves facing and embracing these 'tricky' aspects of ourselves with kindness and understanding. Accepting that there are things that happen to shape who we are, and that we have no choice or control over, can be liberating. That doesn't mean, as we have heard others say, that we are 'letting ourselves off the hook'. Part of self-compassion is also committing to do our best for ourselves and accepting the responsibility for the challenges this endeavour brings.

This felt quite difficult at times, as it involved recognising and engaging with our self-critics. They voiced judgements such as: 'We're the professionals, we should know exactly what to say'; 'It doesn't matter that I have lots of responsibilities and a full diary, I should still feel fully prepared for this group'; 'If people aren't making changes, we're not doing a good enough job!' We found it alarming how loud and entrenched these voices were but also reassuring to realise that our critics drew from the same book when playing on our vulnerabilities. In also sharing our positive experiences of each other, we began to challenge the Critic's narrative.

We began to 'debrief' after group each week and to discuss the foundation of the Critic's assumptions and expectations. We experienced a sadness in realising how dominant our self-critics were and how unchallenged they had been, both by ourselves and by the systems we inhabited. Amongst the many reasons for not previously challenging our Critic, was the influence of our social and cultural contexts. We reflected on how personal achievement and reward seemed to have been strongly valued in our worlds and how this had built an association between imperfection and failure. Whilst we could discuss the other political, social, economic and cultural factors that impacted on the development of our Critic, we did not feel we could do it justice within this chapter!

Through these discussions, the group content and reflecting on our personal practices, we began to notice when our Critic was 'in the driving seat.' In doing so, we also began to develop a new passenger, our imperfect-self. This self acknowledged our 'humanness' and accepted what our Critic considered to be our flaws. It understood our suffering and recognised that we were good enough. In contrast to the Critic's harsh tone, the imperfect-self spoke warmly and kindly of our strengths. It validated our efforts to do our best and encouraged us to own, and even love, our imperfections.

That's not to say that in introducing our imperfect-selves to the driving seat, our Critic was left on the side of the road. After years of determining our speed, direction and destination, it was not happy to relinquish its power. We also realised that we did not necessarily want to banish it. Although the Critic had contributed to a number of our insecurities and self-doubts, it had also led us to strive and achieve. Despite its tenacity, it had served an important function in getting us to where we wanted to be. We spoke about wanting to change our relationship with it, so that our self-critic was acknowledged and embraced as an imperfect part of ourselves.

This might sound like a smooth transition from a mindset dominated by self-doubt to self-compassion. We'd like to say it was. But in reality it's still an ongoing process that takes work and effort on a moment-to-moment basis. Part of this process involved us reflecting on the limits of modelling imperfection in terms of where it sat within the parameters of our professional conduct. We were conscious of the tension between our desire to be human and honest, and our role in containing and guiding the group. We acknowledge that this was an important line to walk and that being 'real' and honest did not necessarily mean disclosing the name of our first pet or the specific details of our innermost fears. Rather it involved being open about our fallibility in a way that felt genuine and safe.

We are aware that despite writing a chapter discussing self-compassion, we have yet to define it. This partly reflects the difficulty of defining something so unquantifiable and also our own reluctance to impose our perceptions on others. The literature defines self-compassion as: 'Compassion directed inward' (Gerner and Neff 2013, p.856); 'recognising when we are struggling, and making a commitment to do what we can to improve things for ourselves' (Welford 2012, p.5); and 'having a healthy stance towards oneself that does not involve evaluations of self-worth' (Neff 2003, in Neff and Vonk 2008, p.25). We have come to operationalise self-compassion as encompassing all of these ideas, and as something that is a process rather than a state activated by that button we were so desperately searching for. Rather than self-compassion being something that we do or do not have, it is a dynamic relationship with ourselves that is affected by a number of different factors at any given time.

Barriers to self-compassion

Self-compassion has been shown to support individuals' resilience, adjustment, wisdom, curiosity, emotional intelligence, social connectedness and reflection (Leary et al. 2007; Heffernan et al. 2010; Neff 2003; Neff, Hseih and Dejitthirat 2005; Neff, Rude and Kirkpatrick 2007; Sbarra, Smith and Mehl 2012). All of these seem like beneficial attributes to develop, which would intuitively support our wellbeing and that of our clients. Research has suggested that staff wellbeing positively impacts upon the therapeutic alliance and client outcomes (Maben et al. 2012). Yet there are numerous challenges in attending to our wellbeing, particularly as practitioners in public healthcare settings.[1]

In developing our own understanding of self-compassion, we have also questioned why such a seemingly obvious and intuitive stance felt so alien and difficult at times. There seemed to be a number of barriers that influenced our ability to show compassion to ourselves. These barriers

---

1   This is likely to apply to other contexts but our professional experience to date has been in the National Health Service (NHS), UK.

existed, and continue to exist, at a personal, relational and cultural level. It is important to be aware of these potential challenges that can get in the way of such a vital practice. We use the word 'vital', because to us, self-compassion is not a phenomenon that might fit some and not others, but rather a philosophy that is integral to our wellbeing and our ability to work at our best. As it is beyond the scope of this chapter to explore every possible barrier to self-compassion, we have chosen to focus on some of those we have experienced or observed in the cultures we work in.

Many of us find ourselves drawn to clinical practice as a result of our compassion for others and a desire to alleviate their distress. In having this focus on other people, we find that our own needs may be overlooked and neglected. The literature often refers to how helping practitioners have played the role of 'rescuer' from an early age (Kottler 2010). This can be considered an understandable pathway into these careers, but can also lead to potentially unhelpful dynamics that we as therapists may experience. Although prioritising the needs of others can fulfil our desire to 'rescue', this is typically done at the expense of attending to our own wellbeing. Of course, whilst this may result in us neglecting some of our needs, the very act of prioritising another may be fulfilling other needs we have. This can make it difficult to notice and adjust these patterns in order to attend to ourselves appropriately. For self-compassion to work, this is a fairly fundamental adjustment to make.

When we have reflected on our own reluctance to prioritise ourselves or resist the need to rescue another, a key emotion that we have discussed is guilt. Whilst multifaceted, such feelings are all fodder for our Critic, who eagerly reminds us that it is our job to 'fix' it. We have noticed this guilt reinforced within the wider narratives of our cultures; we have heard self-care, or self-compassion, referred to as 'selfish', 'a luxury' and 'fluffy'. It is somewhat saddening to read that these have been pervasive attitudes, with Kottler and Blau (1989, p.2) stating that:

> Given the widespread reluctance to discuss mishaps and mistakes, given a professional environment that is suspicious and vigilant, given our self-doubts and the cynicism of an impatient public and disdainful critics, there are few places we can turn to find relief or enlightenment.

Thus, there appears to be a longstanding narrative that highlights a difficulty in getting it 'right' and therefore increases our vulnerability to experiencing blame. In our own journeys, we have noted an archetypal therapist who is always striving to be 'perfect'. Whilst the rational, logical part of us accepted the impossibility of this, another, more childlike part, believed that we should be able to meet these expectations (and that if we could not, we would have failed).

Initially, our realisation that it was okay to be imperfect was accompanied by a sense of relief. Having thought we had let go of our need to achieve perfection, we came to notice that it had been redirected to strive for *perfect imperfection*. That is, that we would model imperfection flawlessly. It took us some time to recognise the irony in this and accept that this was not possible, and to recognise that believing perfect imperfection was attainable posed another barrier to truly practising self-compassion. It is hard to capture the sense of grief and loss that this triggered in us. In genuinely beginning to overcome our belief that perfection was possible, we suddenly found ourselves without a goalpost. Without sounding melodramatic, this insight suddenly called into question a number of our decisions, who we thought we were and what our future held. Unsettling to say the least, but perhaps unsurprising, considering that therapists can feel a strong expectation to be superhuman (e.g. Farber 2000). With this in mind, we have found that seeking help or acknowledging vulnerability, let alone imperfection, can feel somewhat threatening.

Whilst there is a stigma amongst the general population in seeking help or support for emotional distress (Corrigan 2004), research has demonstrated that this can be particularly salient for therapists (Wilson, Weatherhead and Davis 2015). If there is an expectation to be superhuman, or perfect, then acknowledging we are struggling and need support can be equated to failure. There is a perception that we as professionals should be 'sorted' (Wilson *et al.* 2015, p.42) and that this equates to being perfectly and permanently confident and competent. We wonder if there is a fear that engaging in self-compassion portrays us as less competent and undermines our credibility as therapists.

When we have had discussions about self-care with our colleagues, we have noted a number of assumptions regarding the purpose of self-compassion. Whilst some of these were around the benefits of engaging in these practices, many related to a sense that it would be too indulgent to invest in them. We have heard it implied that self-compassion is a means of excusing our faults or mitigating our mistakes, or a way of saying 'there there, never mind' (Welford 2012, p.5). Far from it, a compassionate approach prescribes the need to take responsibility for our actions, and for our growth, whilst acknowledging our limitations and accepting them as part of our common humanity (Patsiopoulos and Buchanan 2011).

There appears to be a misconception that being compassionate to ourselves is as simple as running a bubble bath, lighting candles and eating a mountain of chocolate. Self-compassion may well include running a bath, and even adding bubbles to it; however, the process goes well beyond specific activities or tangible items. It involves: taking a stance of acceptance[2] and not knowing; listening to our inner dialogue with compassion; being mindful; making time for ourselves; and being open about our own fallibility (Patsiopoulos and Buchanan 2011)…easier said than done.

It feels important to acknowledge how much the contexts and cultures in which we are located will affect our opportunity to engage in self-compassion. Both of us predominantly work in the NHS, where delivering care is largely target driven. These pressures have been exacerbated by the current economic and political climates, where productivity is increasingly synonymous with value. We have both had times of feeling that our worth as a member of staff is largely determined by how many clients we have seen, rather than the quality of our work. In this culture, a sense of competition thrives, where level of exhaustion becomes a measure of success. Arguably, at an individual level this culture is perpetuated by our own sense of martyrdom, where we willingly sacrifice our own wellbeing in the name of fulfilling these unachievable targets. This is not a far cry from the rescuer role we discussed earlier. For both of these patterns, we can be drawn into trying to achieve the impossible task of meeting the needs of others before attending to our own.

So, we are other-rescuing, self-denying, superhuman martyrs, with a strong sense of perfectionist-driven guilt, working in pressured environments within a culture that stigmatises self-care as unnecessary indulgence. It is little wonder that our Critic is often the loudest voice that we hear! Our imperfect-self stands little chance against the barriers we face at every level. Nevertheless, the compassionate approach is not to criticise our previous ways of managing these challenges. Rather, it aims to develop our empathy for our Critic and how it became so loud, whilst supporting ourselves to empower a more compassionate-self. For us, an integral part of this process involved the startling recognition that we are not, and never will be, perfect (but that this is okay).

---

2   We are referring to acceptance as a way of seeing things clearly and attending to them with compassion rather than as a tolerance of injustice or a dismissal of distress. For more detailed discussion on this concept see Brach (2003).

Our imperfect-selves

In accepting that we did not need to be perfect, we were suddenly faced with unknown territory. We cautiously started to believe that being 'good enough' was actually good enough. We began acknowledging our own limitations without equating these to failures. It's difficult to describe how liberating this felt. There was sadness in realising how little compassion we had shown ourselves before. Nevertheless, there was also an understanding as to why this had been the case and a hope that with this understanding we could move forward in a different way.

Throughout this process, we have begun to nurture our imperfect-self and to allow others to witness our fallibility. Bellows (2007) suggests that in doing so, we reduce our perfectionist expectations and foster a more realistic self. In turn, clients observe and internalise our modelled self-acceptance and respect. It seems ironic that in doing the things we feared would lead us to be 'lesser' therapists (e.g. accepting our limits, acknowledging our struggles, seeking support), we actually noticed a positive impact on our relationships with clients and with ourselves. Rather than inviting more criticism, our imperfections felt accepted and even welcomed. In wondering why this might be, we reflected on the ability of imperfection to connect us to clients by highlighting our common humanity:

> Common humanity involves recognizing that the human condition is imperfect and that we are not alone in our suffering... We are not alone in our imperfection. Rather, our imperfections are what makes us card-carrying members of the human race. (Gerner and Neff 2013, p.857)

Although it now feels easier to be imperfect than to be always striving for the 'best', this wasn't an easy transition, and it definitely felt uncomfortable initially. Having been conditioned to mask any perceived flaws and aim for perfection, the idea of embracing our insecurities felt fundamentally wrong. Yet we would both highly recommend it! Whilst hard work, it quickly felt, and continues to feel, worthwhile when seeing the impact on both ourselves and those with whom we work.

We would love to offer a concrete formula for developing an imperfect-self, but we believe it is an individual process and one that we are still navigating. Nonetheless, we would like to share some reflections and recommendations on what has helped the process for us. We have summarised these in Figure 1.1, but would emphasise that this is a representation of our journey and not a 'blueprint' for how all imperfect-selves might be cultivated.

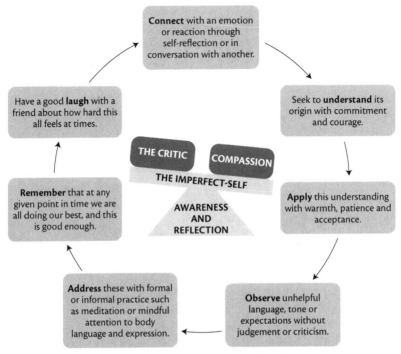

Figure 1.1 Developing our imperfect-selves

One of the key aspects for us has been embracing opportunities to become more mindful of our own reactions and their origins. This has helped us to better understand some of our default responses to challenging situations. One example of this has been writing this chapter. We have repeatedly noticed a desire to produce a 'perfect' chapter and a tendency to second-guess each other's contributions and at times opinions. We noticed that it felt especially exposing to acknowledge our imperfections on paper, which triggered our striving tendencies. In noticing and exploring these responses, we were able to engage our imperfect-self and accept that:

- our reactions were understandable and to be expected

- we appreciated the intention of our Critic to help us achieve the best we could

- our efforts were good enough.

Within the CFT model, Gilbert (2014) discusses the importance of adopting a kind and compassionate tone and facial expression. When we first began practising this, it felt reminiscent of awkward secondary school drama classes – complete with the occasional snigger and sneaking glances at each other. However, we were surprised to see how these seemingly small adjustments impacted our experience of formal compassionate exercises. We experimented with using these in other, less formal, activities – such as writing this chapter. We would strongly recommend attending to the physical aspects of compassion, such as kind and encouraging verbal tones and adopting a small Buddha smile.

As our interest in compassionate practice has developed, we have become more aware of how often our language is blaming, critical or full of judgement. By 'our', we refer not just to the two of us, but also to the wider systems we work and live in. Even when we thought we were being compassionate and mindful of our communication, we often noticed we were using words laden with expectation, such as 'should', 'must' and 'ought'. This has presented an opportunity for the Critic to resurface at times, when we 'failed' to be using the 'right' language. It has also allowed an opportunity for our imperfect-self to engage a non-judgemental, accepting and even humorous attitude towards these reactions.

As we have discussed, the process of believing we are 'good enough' is not a linear one and is not always easy. There have been ups and downs and times when the Critic has been back in the driving seat, particularly in response to looming deadlines. We began talking about 'committing to the process', trusting in ourselves and embracing the belief that we were good enough. This recognition that we were doing our best, given the circumstances of any situation, gave us hope when we needed it. We have also noticed this recognition within clients as a powerful turning point in therapy, where they begin to genuinely hear: 'You are doing your best, and that is enough.'

A common thread throughout this chapter, and our experiences, has been the opportunity to learn from, and lean on, one another. We quickly recognised that comparison was not helpful but that we each had different strengths and capacities for compassion. These were initially easier to notice in each other than in ourselves. Our shared curiosity and openness to developing our imperfect-selves allowed us to reflect on the challenges we noticed in each other's experiences in a non-threatening and encouraging way. We have found that seeking out opportunities to have similar conversations with peers was a helpful starting point, and a necessary support, in developing our self-compassion.

All of these processes have helped us to become more comfortable with modelling imperfection, both in a personal and professional context. We have noted how our colleagues have responded with interest when we have discussed writing this chapter and have been reminded of how alien these concepts can feel. We have found actively modelling our imperfection has been positively received in a variety of settings, from direct work to consultation and supervision. Staff members have commented on how the 'permission' to be imperfect has allowed them to feel more able to be themselves, and consequently be more connected to the team, as well as being able to seek support openly or disclose when they are struggling. Conversely, noticing the impact on others has reinforced our commitment to continuing our self-compassionate practice and the expression of our imperfect-self.

Conclusion

Compassion is not a one-size-fits-all concept, nor can it prevent things from happening that may cause us distress or difficulty. However, it can help us to process and accept those experiences and emotions, and to take responsibility for how we do this. We have noticed 'compassion' become something of a 'buzz word' over recent years, and with this comes a danger of attempting to commodify or pathologise it. Self-compassion is not something that we have or do not have; nor is there something 'wrong' with us if we are struggling to engage with it. As we have discussed, there are numerous barriers to adopting a self-compassionate stance, and many of these are outside our control or choosing. However, we believe that if we can find the courage to acknowledge our imperfections with kindness and understanding, and accept ourselves as good enough, then our lives, and the lives of those around us, will be better for it.

References

Bellows, K. F. (2007). Psychotherapists' personal psychotherapy and its perceived influence on clinical practice. *Bulletin of the Meninger Clinic, 71*(3), 204–226.

Brach, T. (2003). *Radical Acceptance*. London: Random House.

Corrigan, P. (2004). How stigma interferes with mental healthcare. *American Psychologist, 59*(7), 614–625.

Farber, N. K. (2000). Trainees' attitudes toward seeking psychotherapy scale: Development and validation of a research instrument. *Psychotherapy: Theory, Research, Practice, Training, 37*(4), 341–353.

Gerner, C. K. and Neff, K. D. (2013). Self-compassion in clinical practice. *Journal of Clinical Psychology, 69*(8), 856–867.

Gilbert, P. (2010). *Compassion Focused Therapy: Distinctive Features*. London: Routledge.

Gilbert, P. (2014) The origins and nature of Compassion Focused Therapy. *British Journal of Clinical Psychology, 53*, 6–41.

Heffernan, M., Griffin, M. T., McNulty, S. R. and Fitzpatrick, J. J. (2010). Self-compassion and emotional intelligence in nurses. *International Journal of Nursing Practice, 16*, 366–373.

Kottler, J. A. (2010). *On Being a Therapist* (4th edn). San Francisco, CA: John Wiley and Sons.

Kottler, J. A. and Blau, D. S. (1989). *The Imperfect Therapist: Learning from Failure in Therapeutic Practice.* San Francisco: Jossey-Bass.

Leary, M. R., Tate, E. B., Adams, C. E., Allen, A. B. and Hancock, J. (2007). Self-compassion and reactions to unpleasant self-relevant events: The implications of treating oneself kindly. *Journal of Personality and Social Psychology, 92,* 887–904.

Maben, J., Peccei, R., Adams, N., Robert, G. *et al.* (2012). *Exploring the Relationship Between Patients' Experiences of Care and the Influence of Staff Motivation, Affect and Wellbeing.* National Institute for Health Research. Available at www.netscc.ac.uk/hsdr/files/project/SDO_FR_08-1819-213_V01.pdf, accessed on 2 May 2017.

Neff, K. D. (2003). Self-compassion: An alternative conceptualization of a healthy attitude toward oneself. *Self and Identity, 2,* 85–102.

Neff, K. D., Hseih, Y. and Dejitthirat, K. (2005). Self-compassion, achievement goals, and coping with academic failure. *Self and Identity, 4,* 263–287.

Neff, K. D., Rude, S. S. and Kirkpatrick, K. (2007). An examination of self-compassion in relation to positive psychological functioning and personality traits. *Journal of Research in Personality, 41,* 139–154.

Neff, K. D. and Vonk, R. (2008). Self-compassion versus global self-esteem: Two different ways of relating to oneself. *Journal of Personality, 77*(1), 23–50.

Patsiopoulos, A. T. and Buchanan, M. J. (2011). The practice of self-compassion in counseling: A narrative inquiry. *Professional Psychology, Research and Practice, 42*(4), 301–307.

Sbarra, D. A., Smith, H. L. and Mehl, M. R. (2012) When leaving your ex, love yourself: Observational ratings of self-compassion predict the course of emotional recovery following marital separation. *Psychological Science, 23*(3), 261–269.

Welford, M. (2012). *The Compassionate Mind Approach to Building Your Self-Confidence Using Compassion Focused Therapy.* London: Robinson.

Wilson, H. M. N., Weatherhead, S. and Davis, J. S. (2015). Clinical psychologists' experiences of accessing personal therapy during training: A narrative analysis. *International Journal of Practice-based Learning in Health and Social Care, 3*(2), 32–47.

2

Compassion and the Self-Critic

A LIFE-CHANGING, SHARED JOURNEY OF RESILIENCE AND CONNECTION

Dr Liz Tallentire

Clinical Psychologist

I'm a recently qualified clinical psychologist, and I am really pleased to be given this opportunity to share my experiences of compassionate mind training (CMT) with you. This chapter starts with sharing something of my life story. It then goes on to explore how I have shared experiences of compassion in therapy, rewards, difficulties and reflections. I hope that this is presented in a way that is accessible and useful to enable you to apply what I have learnt.

My life journey so far...

My route into clinical psychology training was slightly unusual. I left home aged 16 and initially planned a career as a research scientist. I did A-levels in chemistry, biology, maths and further maths. Following a couple of interviews for lab jobs, I realised this wasn't for me at all! I wanted to work with people, so I came to study an undergraduate psychology degree with the Open University, whilst working and looking after my daughter, who was born when I was 18. During the six years it took to complete my undergraduate degree, life got in the way a little, including getting married, getting divorced (three years later), working full time, looking after my daughter and maybe having some fun too. The outcome was a 2:2. I blamed myself for this and although acknowledging that it had been a difficult time, I thought that I 'should have asked for help'. At this time, Master's-level study was not an option for me due to my financial situation. Therefore, clinical psychology was put on the backburner. I worked as a care assistant, providing personal care and support with household tasks for elderly and disabled people in their own homes, and then as a support worker in adult mental health for six years.

Looking back on this time, I experienced and observed a lot of hardship, but I wouldn't change it if I could. My experiences have helped to make me who I am today. They have given me an insight into the hardship other people have in their lives and how social groups and our life situations can influence and constrain our life choices and our health. In my professional life, my experiences have enabled me to have a genuinely non-judgemental attitude and valuing of others who find themselves in difficulty.

After I completed my degree, I was employed as part of the parent support adviser pilot, which involved working with schools, encouraging parents to participate in their children's learning and supporting families who were experiencing difficulties. I delivered parenting programmes and used approaches based on behavioural and attachment theory. Through this work, I gained a promotion to coordinator, supervising other parent support advisers, and was very fortunate to be given the opportunity to complete a Master's in leadership and management. On this occasion, I applied myself a little better – I was perhaps older and wiser by this point and realised that an opportunity had been given to me – with the result of achieving a distinction. When the parent support adviser funding stream ended, I was redeployed as a manager in Sure Start Children's Centres. This was a difficult transition, as we had all invested so much time and energy in our roles in parent support. With the support of colleagues, and drawing on some previous training relating to endings, I was able to recognise this process as akin to a grieving process. Following mourning the loss of my previous role, I was able to recognise what I had gained: many skills and an opportunity to try something different. Working through this experience helped me to support staff in my team in Sure Start as we experienced round after round of spending cuts with little job security. This was a real challenge to staff morale, and, drawing on my previous experience, I emphasised how important it was to acknowledge and give space to difficult feelings that arose but that with time it could also be seen as an opportunity to make a change. This is an opportunity I took when I decided to apply for clinical psychology training and was successful on my second attempt.

Therefore, I came to clinical psychology training (aged 32 and with a 13-year-old daughter) having never worked as a psychology assistant other than for a few hours of voluntary work but with a broad range of life and work experience. This meant my knowledge of applying specific psychological models was limited, but I had a range of transferable skills and attitudes that would help me, although it took me a little time to realise this. At first, I felt that I was behind other trainees and that I had to start right at the beginning with psychological therapy. As I progressed through training, I gradually recognised the value of my previous experiences, and the characteristics I had previously developed were able to come through: for example, confidence in managing my own work and giving my views, an ability to address difficult issues reflectively, hope and belief in the possibility of change even in the most difficult circumstances and an ability to inspire and motivate others.

Compassionate mind training (CMT) was one of the areas that were new to me. I had some very brief experience with mindfulness practice prior to training, but other than this it was all new. I found that I really related to the combination of compassion with scientific and evolutionary theory (Gilbert 2009). I'd previously thought of myself as quite a compassionate person, and in a lot of ways I was. I could easily see situations from another's point of view and understand why they may get into difficulties. It wasn't until I really started practising compassion that I realised I had a lot more development to do, especially in the area of self-compassion. As with so many of us who choose these high-achieving professions, I could be very understanding of others but very hard on myself and not happy unless I achieved highly. I have now come to recognise this as the part of myself I call my self-critic, who I have playfully characterised as Hyacinth Bouquet. For those of you who are not familiar with the 1990s British TV sitcom *Keeping Up Appearances*, Hyacinth was a character whose surname was actually 'Bucket', but she insisted it was pronounced 'Bouquet'. She spent most of her time trying to give the impression she was upper class, although she was from a working-class family. She was always criticising her family (especially her husband) and telling them what to do. She did care for them deeply and you got the impression that she meant well, despite them being continually irritated by her interfering. Hyacinth has been there throughout my life, for example when I got a 2:2, but I have come to relate to her differently over recent years. I think it's important to recognise this self-critic not as a fault, but as a part of myself that helped me in some ways but could be unhelpful in others. It is what gave me the drive to study, learn and get onto a clinical psychology doctorate. It could be less helpful, however, when it pushed me to achieve at the expense of my own wellbeing and time with my family and insisted that passing wasn't good enough: I had to excel. I soon realised that, when studying at a doctoral level, I needed to make some changes if my health and family were not to suffer significantly, as to achieve the academic standard, to just scrape a pass, was no small feat. To bring this back to my characterisation of Hyacinth, I think of her as meaning well, and I should acknowledge what she says. There's probably something important behind it, she just needs some support to explain it in a more understanding way.

The shared experience of the self-critic in therapy

Alongside noticing these traits in myself, I started to notice certain clients who shared some of these characteristics and for whom Cognitive Behaviour Therapy (CBT) seemed unhelpful or perhaps even damaging. I remember several clients telling me all about their thinking errors and negative core beliefs, and how they felt they had failed, as they were unable to change them. Whilst CBT can be very helpful for many people, I met several of these people who had completed the full offering of CBT and had not improved or had shown little improvement (see Table 2.1).

Table 2.1 Compassionate interpretations of 'problems'

CBT element	My compassionate interpretation
A problem	An experience
A negative automatic thought	A thought
A thinking error	A thinking pattern that may be helpful in some circumstances and less helpful in others
A negative core belief	A belief that forms a fundamental part of who we are, which will probably both help and hinder us
Rule for living	A rule for living that we have developed as an adaptation to our circumstances; again, this will probably both help and hinder us

Something that stood out about these people was the amount of energy they were putting into trying not to experience negative thoughts or feelings. I completed an assessment with one of these people. She had experienced a significant health problem, which had been resolved but left her feeling very anxious, especially about driving. We had recently had several days' teaching in mindfulness and this immediately seemed an appropriate intervention. The client and I made a formulation together, and I explained why I thought mindfulness would be helpful. We, the client and I, recognised that she was so desperately trying to avoid being distressed that she was getting exceedingly anxious about the possibility of getting distressed, and this anxiety was making her distressed. She was then critical of herself for being distressed. I explained that I hoped she could become more accepting of distressing feelings as part of human experience, and, in turn, she wouldn't be so desperate to avoid them; this would then reduce the distress. This seems quite paradoxical – aiming to reduce something by accepting it. I sometimes think of this and explain it as: fighting with distress and trying to avoid thoughts and feelings gives them greater strength. For example, if you try not to think about a pink elephant, you are much more likely to think about a pink elephant than if you didn't try not to think about a pink elephant. Another example, which makes the point in relation to feelings, is to imagine that someone is holding a gun to your head and telling you not to feel frightened because if you feel frightened they are going to shoot you. This sort of control may work in terms of behaviours; we can choose not to act in a particular way, but the same does not apply to feelings and thoughts. Our bodies and minds create these without us choosing their content. We can do things to influence them, but we cannot control them directly.

Compassion practice, rewards and getting stuck

At this point, the client and I agreed she was going to work through a self-help mindfulness book, and we were going to meet again. I had been doing some personal practice but not in a structured way. I decided it was about time I completed a course too. I purchased the book *Mindfulness: A Practical Guide to Finding Peace in a Frantic World* (Williams and Penman 2012) and started to work through the eight weeks of self-guided sessions, which I think took me at least 16 weeks. During this time, I met again with the client, who had made quicker progress than I had. Due to her hard work, she had made significant improvements. She'd stopped giving herself a hard time for being worried about driving into the city; she realised now that this was something many people living in the country found scary, as they don't have to do it very often. She now felt okay about making a decision to get the train instead and was feeling much more confident about driving in general. She really felt the mindfulness she had practised, which included a section on self-compassion, had changed her life.

Following this, I continued with the sessions from the mindfulness book. I became quite stuck at one particular point and realised this was the point when the book focused on self-compassion. I gradually came to realise that the reason I got stuck on this part was because I found it very hard to be compassionate towards myself; whereas my client had quickly developed her compassion, mine was going to take a little longer! My interest in CMT then developed and I started to do some CMT myself. I found the practices very difficult at first but recognised that it was something that would benefit me greatly. I chose to do CMT for my personal development and reflection sessions in the final year of clinical psychology training. I found a particularly helpful exercise was a track recorded by my tutor at university; I think partly because of its accessibility but also because it reminded me of my relationship with her. This has made me realise the benefit of recording tracks yourself for your own clients. Since this time, I have recorded some practices (after I got over cringing at the sound of my own voice) and given clients these as well as ones by other practitioners. So far, all the clients have said they prefer the ones with my voice on them. The practice my tutor had recorded involved visualisation of a compassionate other. I'd created a character, who wasn't based on anyone I knew, and I could bring them to mind in difficult situations, especially when I was feeling sad or having thoughts that I'd failed.

Gradually over time and with practice, I started to notice my relationship with myself changing. I could be kinder to myself when distressed and say to myself 'It is okay that you feel bad'; 'It is understandable in this situation.' When I did this and connected with how I was feeling, I found that my distress didn't last as long. Learning about neural pathways in the brain was a helpful way for me to understand how practice changes things. I'm sure there are much more articulate and educated ways to explain this, but for me it's something like this: we learn things by repeating them, which strengthens the connections between the neurons in the brain that make up the pathways needed for that skill or thought pattern. So the more we practise something, the easier it becomes, because the connections are stronger. Conversely, if we do not use a skill or thought pattern, or have never developed it, the pathways are weaker and more difficult to use.

As my self-compassion developed, I also started to notice a change in my compassion for others. I felt as if it was operating on a different level. Previously, I could understand how others may be feeling; most of the time I was probably operating mainly at a cognitive level. My compassion towards others took on a different quality; it extended to a deeper level of connection, which is hard to put into words. An empathy, not just thought and expressed, but felt deeply through sharing another person's emotions and, in a way, experiencing them with the person. This connection had been there previously to some extent but it now expanded throughout my practice for me to draw upon consciously during sessions. This has some big advantages for the therapeutic relationship, but I have found it also comes with a cost – that of emotional energy. The need for self-care has become even more apparent, especially when working with clients whose identity and emotional states may be fragmented and difficult to integrate and contain (for further discussion see Bateman and Fonagy 2006).

In my final year of clinical psychology training, I did a specialist placement in adult mental health services, working with people who had a diagnosis of personality disorder or other long-standing difficulties. I again came across people who were very hard on themselves and shared some of my traits. I thought the same visualisation technique I had found helpful may be useful for clients I was working with. I soon realised it may be helpful for some people, but it didn't suit everyone, as not everyone can visualise things in their imagination easily. One client who I worked with found it too distressing, as they had chosen someone who had died and then this became muddled with feelings of grief. Working together, this client and I found that a more logical approach worked better for her, for example, by identifying times she was able to show compassion and using this to be compassionate towards herself. She could be kind and compassionate towards a friend she cared about. Therefore, we agreed that when a difficult situation arose, she would say to herself what she would say to that friend if that friend was in the same situation. It was useful to form a step-by-step procedure, agreeing details with the client depending on their needs and preferences. The client writing instructions for themselves may be the most effective way to learn this technique. I have combined it with basic mindfulness and cognitive techniques. For example:

1. Stop – breathe

2. How am I feeling?

    »   Physically?

    »   Emotionally?

    »   How is my mind – is it creating thoughts?

3. Say to yourself what you would say to a friend you care about if they were experiencing these thoughts, feelings and physical feelings. For example:

    »   It's okay and understandable that you feel this way.

    »   It doesn't mean you will always feel this way.

If you or a client found it easier to be compassionate towards yourselves than towards others, then you could swap this round.

Using this technique and modelling of compassion in sessions (towards self and client), this client was able gradually to change her relationship with herself and the difficult experiences she had. I noticed her accounts of events were much less self-critical and more accepting of difficult emotions.

Reflections: CMT has changed my life

I really think that the work I've done using CMT has been one of the most valuable and life-changing elements of clinical psychology training. It has permeated my practice entirely and my life. When I consider the experiences I've had in the last year, I think I have been much more resilient as a result of my practice in compassion. I can experience distress and extremes of emotion, but they don't stay with me for as long. I spend much less time ruminating, especially if I perceive I've made a mistake. I'm able to learn from what has happened and move on. I'm certainly no expert in CMT and I don't think I ever will be, nor do I think that it is important to be. What I do think is important is that I continue to practise being compassionate to others and myself. For me, compassion is not about knowledge; it is about a way of living life. I believe modelling compassion towards yourself and others is the best way for clients to learn it. I have found one of the hardest elements of this is being compassionate about being uncompassionate, both with ourselves and others. For example, this often comes up when you or a client tries compassionate letter writing. You think at the time that you're writing in a really compassionate way, but when it comes to reading it back, especially out loud, you realise it's not as compassionate as you thought. This is okay; it's very difficult to be self-compassionate: the important thing is that you're practising and noticing times when you're not self-compassionate. This process of being compassionate about not being compassionate may be referred to as meta-self-compassion.

Compassion has permeated my work not just when I'm using it directly, but also in my use of other approaches, such as CBT. For example, I refer to 'thinking errors' as patterns of thinking that may be helpful in some circumstances but not others and often link these to evolutionary examples, such as 'black-and-white thinking'. This will be helpful if you work on a production line and have to decide quickly which items to put in the reject bin and which to keep, and it helps me if I use it when sorting out a box of papers and deciding which to keep.

It would also have been helpful in evolution, when thinking about how to escape a wild animal and deciding whether to swim a river or climb a tree. However, in many circumstances it can be unhelpful as it may make us think we only have two options, and we can feel stuck or get caught in cycles of behaviours when there's often a middle, more balanced route that is much more beneficial. A personal example is thinking that I have to either walk right to the top of the fell or not go walking. Either of these options could have positive and negative consequences for my health and how I feel. When I am able to recognise the black-and-white thinking and question it, I am able to recognise other solutions, such as walking halfway or until it feels right to turn around. When I talk to people about core beliefs, I don't describe them as positive or negative but as part of who we are. I suggest that it is not the core beliefs themselves that cause problems but our relationship to them. After all, if we strongly held an opposite core belief, this could be just as problematic. I often use the example of a core belief 'I am a failure': if I thought 'I am a success' and strongly believed this, I could be irritating to others and may not put effort into achieving things, as I would assume I would succeed. I explain that therefore it is not the core belief that we want to change but our relationship to it, often introducing flexibility around it and awareness of how it may influence us. After all, the core belief developed for a good reason and it will have helped us in some ways and will continue to do so. For example, my own core belief of not being good enough, which is entwined with my self-critic (Hyacinth Bouquet) discussed earlier, has helped and hindered me in my life and I am now developing a different, more accepting and skilful way of relating to it.

I'm wondering whether or not to tell you more about my experiences over the past year. Part of me thinks it's a good idea to share that these things happen and that it's okay and possible to get through them, and part of me worries that if you are a trainee clinical psychologist it may fill you with terror. I'll write it down and then decide…

My journey through clinical training went relatively smoothly. I'd completed all assignments on time and passed my placements. There had certainly been stressful times but also a lot of enjoyment and rewards. The first real issue was when I failed my last case report, but this didn't seem too bad, I reasoned, as even if I resubmit and fail again I'll have passed the course (as we were allowed two fails). I negotiated to resubmit this after I'd handed in my thesis, as I could not find room in my mind or schedule for it at the same time. The schedule for my thesis was very tight and I had a few delays finding a field supervisor. However, I worked really hard to get it in on time and was quite happy with it, as were my supervisors. Along came the viva (the final deciding verbal defence of the thesis, which would dictate a pass or fail on the doctorate)! I found it a really difficult experience; the examiners had a number of concerns about my work. I was asked to resubmit and given a year to do so. I made a lot of use of my compassionate imagery and mindfulness at this time and I think this helped me to get over the initial shock, terror and anger much quicker. I was able to tell myself that it was understandable that I felt terrible and like I was a failure (Hyacinth was quite persistent) and was having self-doubting thoughts that I would never qualify as a clinical psychologist. I have since named these self-doubting thoughts Doris Doubt, a name shared by an influential teacher. Accepting these thoughts with compassion, I believe, enabled me to process the experience and move on much more quickly and to produce a plan of how I would achieve this seemingly insurmountable task. I was able to connect with the parts of the work that I enjoyed and experience them in the moment rather than always thinking about the big picture and possible problems it may produce. As it happened, it did produce more problems, but worrying about them wouldn't have prevented them. Towards the end of training, I had been appointed to a Band 8 role (this is a higher paid role than the usual Band 7), but due to the thesis resubmission, I was not able to apply for a Health and Care Professions Council (HCPC) registration and therefore was unable to take up the post. Following some discussion, the employer agreed to appoint me at a lower rate of pay for a temporary, six-month contract. I enjoyed my job during this time. I worked four days a week, but it was not an easy job and I had a lot of travelling. I realised that I needed to pace my thesis work, as I would have to maintain it for some time due to the amount I had to do. So I steadily worked away on the thesis during set hours two days a week. Well, it's amazing how quickly six months goes, and whilst the thesis was progressing, it was clear I would not have HCPC registration before my contract ended. Unfortunately, my employer was unable to renew the temporary contract and I found myself out of work. Naturally, self-critical thoughts and worries arose: 'I should have seen this coming'; 'I should have looked for another job'; 'How am I going to pay the bills?' (Doris Doubt and Hyacinth Bouquet again). Amazingly, and I say amazingly because I'm still genuinely surprised by it, I didn't get caught up in these thoughts for long. I acknowledged them and told myself it was understandable that I was having them and they reduced. I thought to myself: 'What will happen will happen, all I can do is try my best.' I set out a plan of applying for jobs and spending time on my thesis, which was now nearing completion (although it didn't feel that way at the time). To get myself out of the house, I spent some time helping on my friend's farm and really enjoyed this. About a month later, I was successful in gaining a post as a mindfulness practitioner, training staff across two NHS trusts. This is my current post and I am thoroughly enjoying it. Just yesterday I received the news that my resubmitted thesis has been 'awarded forthwith', passed with no amendments. I'm still struggling to believe this is true; surely there must be some typos (there's Hyacinth again, ha ha).

Parting words

I hope this story conveys that sometimes difficult things happen; sometimes we fail at things that mean a lot to us, and that's part of life. It is okay to fail and it is okay to carry on or not to, depending on what's best for you at that time. We can bring self-compassion to these failures and recognise them not as something that reflects something intrinsic about us, but as events on the journey through life that make us who we are and perhaps make us more resilient and more able to share the difficulties of others who we work with. We can model that it's okay to have these really difficult thoughts and emotions: to be sad or angry, to cry, to blame yourself – we don't have to hide these emotions away from others or from ourselves. We can experience them as part of life, as part of a life that is full and varied, a life that is really lived, not for what was and what may be, but for this moment. We then gain a different perspective, a kindness in our approach. This does not mean we never plan for the future nor strive to improve but that we do this whilst recognising our experiences on the journey. Connecting with what it's like to be on the journey – often when we do this and accept the negative thoughts and feelings, we realise that much of the journey is not as bad as we thought and in fact may be quite enjoyable.

The worksheets that follow this chapter offer some practical tips and guidance as to how we can begin to introduce a compassionate outlook and self-kindness into our day-to-day life experiences.

References

Bateman, A. and Fonagy, P. (2006). *Mentalization-based Treatment for Borderline Personality Disorder*. Oxford: Oxford University Press.

Gilbert, P. (2009). *The Compassionate Mind: A New Approach to Life's Challenges*. Oakland, CA: New Harbinger Publications.

Williams, M. and Penman, D. (2012). *Mindfulness: A Practical Guide to Finding Peace in a Frantic World*. New York: Rodale.

COMPASSION WORKSHEET 1 – SELF-KINDNESS

Stop – breathe	
What is the situation?	
I'm about to do a presentation on my research in front of about 30 people	
How am I feeling?	
Physically	Tension in chest, arms and legs, neck and back, stomach churning
Emotionally	Anxious, afraid
In my mind	Persistent self-critical and doubting thoughts (Hyacinth and Doris Doubt)
What would you say to a friend you care about if they were experiencing these thoughts, feelings and physical feelings?	
It's okay and understandable that you feel this way It doesn't mean you will always feel this way I'm here if you need me I know it feels really important now, but it is not the end of the world if it goes wrong	

COMPASSION WORKSHEET 2 – THINKING PATTERNS

Our brains are always looking for more efficient ways to process information. A lot of the time this is really helpful but sometimes it can get in the way too. It can be useful to recognise the patterns our brains are using at different times. The table below gives some examples of common thinking patterns and situations in which they may be helpful or unhelpful. You may see these patterns elsewhere with different names; the names are not as important as recognising the pattern.

Name	Description	Possibly helpful circumstance	Possibly unhelpful circumstance	Possible alternative
All or nothing thinking/ categorical thinking	If it's not one thing it must be another, no in between. Often related to decision making	Working on a production line, deciding which products to reject. Running away from a wild animal and deciding whether to climb a tree or swim a river	Making a decision about a career change. Assessment of others' actions	What are the shades of grey? Are there any in-between options?
Catastro-phising	Thinking that the worst possible thing will happen	Keeping you safe, doing risk assessments	Going on holiday thinking it's all going to go wrong so not enjoying it	Assessing the actual level of risk, deciding if this is okay for you
Mental filtering or dark glasses	Only acknowledging information/ sensations of one type, often negative	Noticing defects during quality control	During leisure activities, only noticing what goes wrong	Paying attention to your experience in the moment – mindfulness practice
Mind reading	Thinking that you know what someone else is thinking	If lightly held, guessing what others might be thinking in a social situation can be helpful	Assuming an action of another means they are thinking something specific	Asking others their opinion
Over gener-alising	Making an assumption based on a small number of incidents	Having been bitten by two snakes when standing on them, assuming that snakes will bite if you stand on them	Having met two people from London who were rude, assuming all people from London are rude	Being open to other possibilities

COMPASSION WORKSHEET 3 – COMPASSIONATE PRACTITIONING

Experience	Thought(s)	Consequences
Becoming nervous about doing a presentation, noticing heart racing and breathing increasing	I can't do it I'm no good at presentations I'm going to mess it up Thinking patterns used in thought(s) (see worksheet 2) Over generalising, filtering, catastrophising, all-or-nothing thinking Alternative thoughts outside of these thinking patterns It doesn't have to be perfect, I'm usually good enough at presentations even if I am nervous It's okay to be nervous. If it goes wrong it's not the end of the world	Emotions: Fear, panic Body sensations: Heart beating hard, body tense, breathing difficult, flushed, shaking Actions: Mumbling, talking fast, making mistakes Possible consequences of these alternative thoughts: Emotions: Nervous Body sensations: Less extreme Actions: Clearer speech, slowing down, able to think and carry on if mistakes made

3

Compassion Across Cultures

Dr Caroline Wyatt, Dr Olivia Wadham,
— Dr Amy D'Sa and Ndumanene Devlin Silungwe —
The Umoza Trust

The authors of this chapter are trustees of UK-based charity The Umoza Trust. Dr Caroline Wyatt, Dr Olivia Wadham and Dr Amy D'Sa are all clinical psychologists who trained at Lancaster University. During their training, they recognised the importance of cross-cultural collaborations and the value that these experiences could add to their own clinical work in the UK. They arranged innovative specialist placements abroad in Eastern Africa (Malawi and Uganda) during the final year of their training, an experience that allowed them the space to reflect on Western understandings of mental health and, importantly for this chapter, compassion within a mental health context. Currently, all three authors work in UK-based clinical settings within the NHS and private services (NHS adult eating disorder services, children's homes and NHS child and adolescent mental health services respectfully). Their shared interest is in improving psychological understanding of mental health, recognising in this the importance of shared experiences and learning. This ethos underpins their charity and clinical work.

Currently, The Umoza Trust focuses on developing a project with St John of God Services in Malawi, and a visit to Malawi in May 2016 provided an opportunity to pose the question: 'What does compassion mean across cultures?' When considering how to explore the answers to this question, we immediately knew that we could not write this chapter alone. Although we have seen many examples of what we understand as compassion during our work in Malawi, we are certainly in no position to speak for those who live such very different lives to our own.

We invited our friend and colleague Ndumanene Devlin Silungwe to co-author this chapter because of his identity as both a born-and-bred Malawian and one of the country's few psychologists. Devlin works as a clinical psychologist within St John of God Services conducting psychosocial assessments and designing interventions at individual, group and family levels in the child and adult mental health services. Devlin also teaches psychology and human development courses at the St John of God College of Health Sciences and participates in the clinical supervision of students pursuing a Diploma in psychosocial counselling. His interests are in the place of faith in coping with chronic physical and mental health conditions, neglect and abuse of children and enhancement of positive parenting skills.

In writing this chapter with Devlin, we expected to find similarities and differences in our conceptualisation and experiences of compassion and wanted to represent these diverse perspectives fully rather than try to combine them into a single narrative. We therefore decided to write this chapter as a summary of themes that were reflected in conversations, shared experiences and email communication between the authors. We use examples from these to illustrate each of the themes. The opportunity to be part of these conversations was a sincerely humbling and emotive experience, and we hope you will experience some of this too.

The following themes consider how we engage with compassion and how this is a personal and professional challenge. We particularly aim to explore what compassion means and how this connects with the culture it is experienced within or between.

'Total immersion' and the concept of Ubuntu

When exploring definitions of compassion within Malawian culture, it became apparent that compassion signified an intense experience of 'total immersion' from the perspective of the person offering compassion to another.

Devlin: I would say that one of the contexts in which you are likely to see compassion being expressed is during bereavement, during severe illnesses; during any kind of suffering, in a context where you'd say you can touch suffering with a finger, if there was a way to touch it. You are definitely likely to see compassion being expressed. It's really some kind of wanting to be immersed with the feeling of someone, or something that someone is going through. Wanting to feel almost as if you are actually the one going through that particular experience. And maybe wanting to take away the suffering from them.

The Umoza Trust (UT): I'm reminded of how compassion is often defined in the UK, as an awareness of the suffering of ourselves and other people, and a commitment to relieve this (Gilbert 2010). It seems as though in Malawi, there is also an emphasis on wanting to take that suffering from them?

Devlin: To me, compassion is really total immersion, becoming part of the suffering of another person and wishing you could actually transfer that, if possible, you would actually be the one experiencing it other than them; and asking the questions: 'Why should it be you, it didn't need to be you, I wish it would be different from what is happening now.' Also, it's about saying this is not something you would wish anybody to experience. It is like they are going through an experience from the position of the conscious self, I feel this difficulty, I have sensations about it; you may either acknowledge this, not be aware about it or even minimise it by reassuring yourself that things are fine, it's not a problem. I would say that would be my understanding.

This exchange captures the intense and overwhelming nature of offering compassion to another, by truly sharing that experience with them, in that moment. The description of being able to 'touch suffering with a finger' conveys the strength of this and the experience of one's proximity to another's suffering. There is an additional sense of people's willingness to almost sacrifice their own happiness to relieve the suffering of another.

Devlin also expressed the concept of truly sharing suffering with another through his use of language, often using plural pronouns such as 'we' when talking about compassion.

UT: I noticed that you use 'we' when you talk about experiencing compassion; is it something that is very much a collective experience in Malawi?

Devlin: You know, we have a 'we' psychology in Malawi, it's a collective psychology. The suffering of one is always the suffering of everybody and that has actually shaped quite a lot the way relationships work, in particular when it comes to issues of suffering. So I would say that is fundamental, we've grown up mostly not thinking of my needs first, but always being able to think 'our' needs, not my, but our needs. I would give an experience of the compassion of grief. Where you are able to feel the loss that someone else has gone through, it almost always leads to an outpouring of grief not just for the person but for yourself. So, you are able to get as much attached as they are about a situation. I'm sure that definitely brings relief to the person who feels supported. The feeling that they are not feeling it alone, that you are also feeling with them. Whatever they are feeling, you are also. This outpouring of grief, crying and all that, to share that, it's something that you are feeling together.

This description of the collective culture and consideration of 'our needs' is reminiscent of the concept of Ubuntu (uMunthu in Malawi), which widely influences African culture. Ubuntu is the 'capacity in African culture to express compassion, reciprocity, dignity, harmony and humanity in the interests of building and maintaining community with justice and mutual caring' (Nussbaum 2003, p.2); ultimately it is the philosophy that 'my pain is your pain; my wealth is your wealth; your salvation is my salvation' (Nussbaum 2003, p.2). This sharing of experiences through interconnectedness is likely a powerful experience for those experiencing suffering or distress due to the strong sense of togetherness, belonging and connection that Ubuntu enhances. As trustees of The Umoza Trust, we feel incredibly privileged to have experienced this within Malawian culture. We have warm memories of a lady we met during her time as an inpatient in a mental health hospital, who often sang to us the lyrics 'I am because you are; you are because I am.' During the same visit, a fellow client held our hands and shared their belief that we 'are two colours, but one people'.

This social philosophy is in contrast to the individualist culture we have experienced within the UK, where personal achievements and successes are generally valued above group or collective efforts. When considered within the 'three systems model' of compassion-based approaches (see Paul Gilbert's publications), it could be suggested that Western cultures activate the 'threat' and 'drive' systems more consistently, creating a competitive culture with less value placed on the affiliative aspects of our soothing system. In the collectivist culture of Malawi, perhaps accessing compassion through connection with others is a more inherent and natural process. During our discussions with Devlin, he explored this idea, as well as his thoughts on how we develop the capacity to be compassionate.

Devlin: …I believe it [compassion] is an inherent adaptive human emotion that develops very early in intra- and interpersonal relationships. While one can feel compassionate with the inanimate world, it is with the animated life of humans that this is truly expressed. It is like you are saying 'I have received this before; people have given this to me when I was in need.' You're trying to give back what you have received through others being compassionate to you. I definitely believe that for any average human being, compassion should come naturally, beginning with the early mother–child reciprocal attuned manner of relating. It might be induced, yes, but it's something that has naturally been experienced.

Here Devlin describes how one's capacity to express compassion is dependent upon our prior experience of compassion from others, highlighting the inherently relational and reciprocal nature of compassion. This idea also echoes attachment theory (Bowlby 1969) in that our early experiences of relating to our caregivers provide a template for how we relate to others, including how we express compassion within relationships and towards ourselves. Within our clinical work, we often observe barriers to self-compassion that appear to mirror early messages received from caregivers, for example judgements about feeling and expressing distressing emotions can result in guilt or shame later in life when distress is experienced. In Malawian culture, care is often seen to be provided by the extended family and wider community, perhaps developing a community sense of how compassion is usually displayed. Devlin suggested that people who express compassion outside of this norm might be viewed as lacking in compassion.

Devlin: All of us are compassionate I'm sure; it's really the degree to which we can actually express it. I believe that that is an evolutionary feature of being human, but I guess there are some people that are more compassionate, there are others that are less compassionate. So if we have a continuum I wouldn't really say zero to a maximum – whatever this could be, but it might just be that others have a different way of expressing it.

This implies that everyone is capable of compassion in some form, as this is part of being human. However, perhaps compassion can be expressed in different ways depending on our experiences of this from others.

Self-compassion

When discussing compassion, there is often an emphasis on compassion from and to others, with less recognition of compassion towards oneself. We discussed this with Devlin to understand self-compassion within Malawian culture.

UT: One of the things that is noticed in the UK is that people are often very good at expressing compassion towards others, but struggle with being compassionate towards themselves; is that something you notice in Malawi?

Devlin: Yes, I would most always be surprised if people actually take time to be compassionate to themselves. Normally that's very difficult, suffering is always seen in others, but when it is yourself, no. We are naturally attuned, I believe, to experiencing the burden in others when that involves a threat to their survival. Probably self-compassion happens at the level where you don't know that you're doing it, so let me say that it would happen, but because you are too used to externalising compassion, then you'll not even know that you are actually doing it to yourself. So, it happens but it's almost unconscious. Mostly it's expressed outwards, towards others.

Here, Devlin conceptualises compassion towards others as a natural evolutionary urge, perhaps developed as part of the system that facilitates the connections and social relationships that are crucial to our survival. In contrast, self-compassion seems to be more difficult to define, and considered to be an unseen or unconscious process. In some respects, this parallels our experiences within the UK, where being compassionate towards our own self is often viewed as selfish or self-indulgent. Although in the UK people are often encouraged to think about self-compassion in a superficial sense (e.g. buying beauty products because 'we are worth it'), we are not always encouraged to be authentically compassionate towards ourselves. However, the lack of compassion towards self could be seen to be a more conscious decision for people within the UK, rather than the 'almost unconscious' process described by Devlin.

The burden of compassion

Devlin explained that compassion towards others is often expressed more overtly through actions; for example, by visiting or calling a person in demonstration that you are holding them in mind – 'being away and yet present within them in your connection with their situation'. He went on to explore the experience of receiving such compassion.

Devlin: I believe that sometimes compassion overwhelms those you are providing the compassion to. I guess the person who is experiencing it senses the burden sometimes that their condition is leaning on those who are accompanying them during that moment in which they are suffering.

UT: So the person receiving compassion can sometimes perceive this as a burden to the other?

Devlin: Yes, very much so. I guess there is a moment where you realise that the suffering is taking a toll on them but pain is also being reflected on you, who has to be present. It is two-way; you are feeling with and becoming them. You see how it feels for them; if it feels this way for you, you can appreciate how terrible it is. Maybe the immersion I talked about gets to be communicated as in a mirror and since compassion is reciprocal, it is possible for the one suffering to feel scared about it, choked, smothered and even fearful for the emotional strain it has on the one providing it.

The suggestion here is that while one is empathising with the suffering of another, this empathy is also reflected back, so the person suffering becomes concerned that there is an emotional burden on the person who is sharing in their experience. This concept links with the literature around carer burden within the UK, although this is often associated with home care situations involving only primary caregivers (e.g. Etters, Goodall and Harrison 2008). Perhaps the collectivist culture within Malawi leads to a wider network of 'carers' and more widespread carer burden; while the disadvantage to this is the number of people who may experience some form of burden from one's suffering, the advantage may be that the burden is shared and may therefore be more manageable. However, the sense of burden may also be more apparent within Malawian culture due to the expectation of compassion as being part of the collectivist or Ubuntu philosophy.

Devlin: …this relates to 'the expectation to express it or show it in some way'. You might be compassionate or you might find yourself not being as compassionate as somebody is expecting you to be. Maybe one person who I am very close to is not visiting; there is a possibility to see this as lack of concern for what I'm going through. I guess they are likely to conclude that you're not compassionate. When in accuracy it might be that you are compassionate, but there is just something that is actually sitting in between that expression for them to know you've been compassionate. But where they don't see or the expectation of how you must be compassionate and you're not, they are likely to have a different interpretation that can hurt the relationship.

This highlights how there is a clear expectation within Malawian culture to show compassion through actions. This can create a pressure on caregivers; in the absence of showing compassion, they may risk ruptures in their relationships or be perceived by their community as uncaring.

Compassion fatigue and barriers to compassion

Devlin also noted that there are times when people can struggle to connect with compassion for another, which he described as 'negative compassion'.

> Devlin: But it [compassion] may also be unnoticed where the person is too overwhelmed or angry with the situation of another to acknowledge; expressed instead in being distant, withdrawn, or a denial of the feelings. Negative emotions towards self, resulting in dysfunction, are a possible indication of negative compassion.

This seems to echo the notion of compassion fatigue, an experience increasingly acknowledged and discussed in the UK (e.g. Newell and MacNeil 2010). Put simply, this is when one's ability to express compassion towards others diminishes, often due to the overwhelming levels of stress or distress they have experienced through being compassionate. During our time in Malawi, we noticed that clients demonstrating high levels of emotional distress were often managed through being moved away from others or distracted, perhaps reducing the opportunity for staff to provide active listening or comfort. We have noticed in the UK that clients often look for distractions to push away painful feelings; perhaps as professionals we can also struggle to sit with and connect with this discomfort.

Devlin talked about key barriers that can make being compassionate more difficult, and perhaps therefore make compassion fatigue more likely. These barriers included: 'where the person that you have to express compassion with is also somebody that might have hurt you' or 'when there are certain issues that are of a social justice or human rights nature, for which they are in trouble or suffering...for example a drug trafficker, rapist or perpetrator of murder being imprisoned, sick or on death row'. It seems that these issues create a distance within relationships and make it much more difficult for one to empathise with their situation.

A further barrier to compassion involves the various beliefs around mental health within Malawi. Mental health difficulties in individuals are commonly attributed to drug or alcohol use.

Devlin: There is a strong belief among some Malawians that many mental illnesses among males are caused by drug abuse and the belief that these people may have been warned about their risky behaviour before the onset. Thus, where caregivers and communities may interact with the patient on their bad habits, the expression of compassion would be reduced due to this history. Before the mental health difficulties, the family might have told the person not to take drugs, and it might be difficult for them to experience compassion for that person later.

This echoes our experience whilst in Malawi. When patients disclosed any drug use, this was often used as the primary reason for their mental health difficulties, with less weight given to previous traumatic histories. In our experience, the reasons why someone may have used drugs or alcohol were rarely explored. We wondered whether drugs and alcohol may have been a coping mechanism for more significant difficulties many of these individuals were experiencing. These experiences have some similarities with attitudes towards mental health within the UK, where substance use is often separated from mental health difficulties and can be perceived as a lifestyle choice, which somebody can change, potentially reducing expressed compassion.

Another common belief around mental health within Malawi involves ideas of witchcraft. The spiritual beliefs of many Malawians can lead them to attribute mental health difficulties (or any unusual behaviour by an individual) to witchcraft – the implication being that the person has done something that has led them to be cursed. Unfortunately, this can lead to significant stigma and a practice of out-casting the individual with mental health difficulties. Alternatively, individuals may be subjected to spiritual practices or rituals in an attempt to rid them of the 'curse'. Although such practices are culturally accepted, comments from those who have experienced them suggest that they can themselves be traumatising. Understanding where distress comes from and what contributes to distress influences expressions of compassion. As part of psychological practice, we are used to viewing psychological formulation as a vital component of working with a client so they can feel heard and supported. Alternative attributions, or a lack of understanding, seem to maintain stigma around mental health difficulties in both Malawi and the UK, getting in the way of compassion being felt and experienced.

Devlin described how understanding mental health difficulties as witchcraft may sometimes increase compassion from those close to the patient, as they express anger towards the potential perpetrator (i.e. whoever initiated the curse). However, he also recognised how this can hold a greater 'emotional burden' as 'no one wants to see their relative reduced in their behaviour to a near non-human'. The notion of a patient being somehow less human when experiencing mental health difficulties may reflect the unfamiliarity of these behaviours to most Malawians; this unfamiliar and therefore potentially unnerving presentation may create a further barrier to compassion.

Separating personal and professional compassion

For us as professionals who work with people with mental health difficulties on a daily basis, these presentations are not so unfamiliar. Devlin talked, however, about how a different approach to compassion was required in professional settings in comparison to in one's personal life.

Devlin: Compassion is to remain, you don't disengage, you really are present. I guess there can be a split between personal and professional expressions of compassion. For me, compassion in my personal life is total immersion, becoming part of the suffering of another person and wishing you could remove it from them. It would go against what you would say is a therapeutic experience, where you are not allowed to take the pain and the suffering of somebody and have it.

UT: So compassion can be expressed differently at work than in your personal life?

Devlin: I think the clinical training itself played a role in modifying how I believe I should express compassion. I think it gave me an awareness of the difference between compassion and empathy. Sometimes there is a conflict, where you truly know that this is a situation that you might begin to literally feel with somebody.

This separation of expressing empathy in professional settings and compassion in personal life is interesting, along with the suggestion that clinical training somehow 'modifies' the natural compassionate response in order to enhance its therapeutic nature. It seems that compassion with a desire to take one's suffering away is considered less therapeutic, perhaps in acknowledgment of how this creates a 'rescuing' dynamic with the power firmly with the person who 'rescues' the other. Indeed, this is similar to our understanding of therapeutic relationships within the UK, which encourage connection and collaboration, ultimately empowering the client to find solutions to their own difficulties. The difference between compassion and empathy is explored further below.

Devlin: If I went away [from work] and continued to think about it, I would have entered into the realm of compassion and it would have stopped being empathy. Empathy at work is okay, 'I feel how you are and we are going to work through it', and then after that 'Thank you, but it was just work.' It's always a fine line though because as human beings, we are meant to be compassionate I believe, which is something I do especially when I am dealing with the people who are closer to me. Compassion is a continuum: it's most fully taken up when you are with the people who are closest to you. I think compassion is not something encouraged in the context of work in our profession! It is something that has been left in the realm of the home or faith, with me and my close relatives. For my professional self, I need something that allows me to disengage and be able to say 'Okay, I've done what I needed to do and that is it', especially because unlike in ordinary relationships, stories and situations of hurt or pain are a daily occurrence in the life of doctor–patient or client–therapist relationships.

The idea of professional empathy suggests that some level of 'disengagement' is crucial in client–therapist relationships. This almost acts as a protective mechanism, reducing potential emotional burden on the therapist. There appears to be a striking difference between Devlin's experience of compassion within his personal and professional life; we wondered whether the influence of Western thinking on psychological training might help us to understand this. Although compassion is one of the core values of the UK National Health Service, there is also recognition that remaining compassionate can be at the detriment of professionals' own emotional wellbeing and can, over time, lead to 'burnout' or 'compassion fatigue'. The protective nature of the 'professional empathy' described is explored further below.

Devlin: I think we also cannot move our personalities out of this, as well. You're likely to have some people who are likely to pour out more of the compassionate approach than others. I guess I am one of the compassionate side, maybe because it's also part of our culture and faith. We grow up, I believe, with the model of compassion being part of being a human being. Then the profession brings us to the awareness of empathy as a protective shield against getting overwhelmed because of the nature of the work mental health providers do – seeing and hearing pain and suffering.

The idea of empathy as a protective shield is worthy of note, suggesting this shield is used to intentionally prevent professionals from expressing compassion in order to avoid 'total immersion' in the suffering of another. It seems this is used as a therapeutic tool to potentially avoid a rescuing dynamic but also to reduce emotional burden on the clinician. Whilst this approach contrasts with UK services where compassion is encouraged, it may protect clinicians from experiencing compassion fatigue by creating safe distance in the therapeutic relationship, without losing empathy.

It seems that these cross-cultural collaborations have the power to offer important mutual learning. The 'we' culture described, as witnessed during our time in Malawi, is testament to the immersive nature of being compassionate through 'feeling with' someone. To do so is to connect and be alongside, generating a feeling of belonging that is healing in itself. This is a wonderful and powerful message for us to receive in the UK both within services and in society. It seems essential that people are heard and that compassion is shown through our words and actions. In our professional role, this creates a challenge where we must find a way of authentically expressing empathy and compassion regardless of the person's history and whilst holding our own emotional needs in mind. It supports the idea of working alongside our clients as 'experts by experience' and we hope that the increasing emphasis on involving clients within their own care and within service development may help us to feel more of a 'we' than a 'them and us'.

We believe the African beliefs and values discussed in this chapter have a lot to contribute to our understanding of compassion, but also to efforts to enhance compassion across services and within Western society more widely. Further projects to support mutual learning across countries and cultures, such as those supported by The Umoza Trust, are crucial in supporting culturally sensitive practice and developing services globally.

References

Bowlby, J. (1969). *Attachment and Loss: Attachment*. London: Hogarth Press.

Etters, L., Goodall, D. and Harrison, B. E. (2008). Caregiver burden among dementia patient caregivers: A review of the literature. *Journal of the American Academy of Nurse Practitioners, 20*(8), 423–428.

Gilbert, P. (2010). *The Compassionate Mind*. London: Constable.

Newell, J. M. and MacNeil, G. A. (2010). Professional burnout, vicarious trauma, secondary traumatic stress, and compassion fatigue: A review of theoretical terms, risk factors, and preventive methods for clinicians and researchers. *Best Practices in Mental Health, 6*(2), 57–68.

Nussbaum, B. (2003). African culture and Ubuntu: Reflections of a South African in America. *Perspectives, 17*(1), 1–12.

PART TWO

Living with Compassion and Inviting Others

Reactions are the probable product of hardship which we should empathise with but need to be addressed in order that we use a fully compassionate approach, that is not just being soft, warm and empathetic, but also being assertive to move forward with responsibility and a will to improve situations.

Kirsten Atherton

4

Working with Compassion in CAMHS

Dr Kirsten Atherton
Clinical Psychologist

When you think of vulnerable people in society, children must not be far from the top of your list, if not at the top. So some may wonder why using compassion when working in child and adolescent mental health may be more challenging at times than expected.

> *The softest things in the world overcome the hardest things in the world.*
>
> Lao Tzu

I discuss compassion in terms of an approach or attitude to others but also as a form of therapy. In this chapter I will discuss my understanding of how compassion can be applied though systemic work, directly with children and as therapists, in an environment of a child and adolescent mental health team (CAMHS).

Systems

The system a child exists within may be minimal or extensive. The two systems I will discuss are the healthcare services around a child and the child's family.

> *When a flower doesn't bloom, you fix the environment in which it grows, not the flower.*
>
> Alexander Den Heijer

Services around a child

A child's safety, and therefore ability to feel and to be safe, along with developing feelings of security, is central to working with a compassionate approach. In my mind, the first and foremost job for the system around a child is to try to keep the child safe. As practitioners, we are trained to consider safety as a multifaceted concept when working with vulnerable people. Threats from physical, psychological and emotional sources present in many ways for young people. In CAMHS, we think a lot about safety and risk to children, both in internal and external terms. For example, is the child behaving in a way that could harm themselves and is the child in a safe environment? Outside of our direct clinical work with a child or young person, our assessment of risk and safety can be extensive. Maslow's 'Hierarchy of Needs' (1943) explains that it would be difficult to do higher-order thinking, for instance to engage in therapeutic psychological work, if your basic need for safety is not met. It may not be appropriate to think about cultivating feelings of safeness if responding to threat stimuli is an important reality to a child.

Before even meeting a child, the assessment begins from the referral pathway and the information included. We must assess systems around the child through the lens of child protection. Critical risk aside, referrals are often not accepted by CAMHS due to the child's environment not being stable or safe enough to allow a fair assessment of what may be extreme psychological distress, what would be an appropriate level of difficulties given the circumstance and what is a serious mental illness. An example may be of a junior-school-aged child who is referred because their behaviour in the school environment is perceived to be unusual and worrying; they are drawing dark images and speaking of death and destruction. Included in the referral information is a report stating that the child has made allegations of physical assault by a parent. Social workers are reported to be currently investigating the allegation and whilst the child was initially removed to another family member's house for a week, they have since been returned to their family home. We could naturally understand from the behaviours described that the child is communicating a level of psychological distress, but, given the additional information, is there any indication that this is abnormal for a child in this situation or any suggestion that the child has a mental illness or requires assessing for a 'problem' in the first instance?

Suitable timing is often the key to our work. Unfortunately, this is sometimes compromised by waiting lists and service restrictions but also, occasionally, readiness for therapeutic input can be enhanced by a wait. In the described situation, the fundamental need for the child is to be in an environment that they consider predictable and safe, where their needs are considered and heard. These scenarios often lead to difficult conversations with social workers, school nurses or others who may have concerns about the child and would appreciate CAMHS 'fixing' the child, because it is clear there is something wrong. A great amount of the work for children in these situations can be done though the system around a child. Sadly, frequently the family environment is one of chaos, unpredictability, threat and inconsistency. Systems of social work, education and health services should still mobilise for these children, to help provide security, support and boundaries, but often social workers have the more substantial role.

In my current service, a forum to think together with social workers has been established to have a space to bring difficult 'stuck' cases, or cases they have concerns about, which may not initially have been accepted to CAMHS assessment for reasons previously described. Our awareness of child development and trauma is used to develop a formulation and help consider a child and family's needs. The forum allows exploration of the experience of working with the family, which can often be informative, and explanations and application of theories of developmental trauma and the effects on the developing brain. Delivering the message that stability, predictability and continuity are paramount in a child's environment to help promote their feelings of safety is often a fundamental part of working with the systems around the child. It also enables an opportunity for systems around the children to understand the feelings they can have evoked by working with a particular family. Considering and helping the practitioners to understand the processes involved in these cases increases the possibility of positive outcomes. Often, increasing understanding and perspective taking, in addition to cultivating compassion, can be really important and useful interventions at these times to increase the productivity of the system and its ability to work with the family. The forum also allows a more informed holistic assessment of a case and can act as a referral if a child discussed is identified as an appropriate case for CAMHS due to changes in circumstance or with the addition of further information.

These interactions can provoke frustration or challenges when faced with external professionals' demands about the role of CAMHS and a need for a child to be seen. In my mind, I can be honest and recognise that the feelings we are being shown by other agencies are those we might experience when we are concerned for the families we see and, at times, when we are frustrated by the system. We must recognise this as the manifestation of their concern and contain their anxiety by explaining the plan for the child and other supports available in the meantime.

Using the compassion-focused approach, we need to build our own compassion for the other professionals by recognising their suffering, that is their feelings of being overwhelmed by a case or their workload, and noticing their desperation for help. In my experience, this allows me to contain my reaction to how the professional treats me and allows me to engage with their struggle, meaning I can help them move forward rather than being caught in the experience of their often negative presentation. We then must try to hold their concerns whilst scaffolding their ability to think through alternative strategies. By helping the cultivation of compassionate motivation by thinking through a formulation of the situation, practitioners are empowered and understand that they can take responsibility for coordinating appropriate care for families. The care they go on to provide is a gesture of commitment to try to alleviate and prevent further difficulties for the families.

The child's family

Being deeply loved gives you strength; loving deeply gives you courage.

Lao Tzu

It is important to recognise that there are some incredibly resourceful families and parents in our service – those who engage openly and honestly and work hard for their children. As a clinical psychologist, but also just as a person, I have an absolute respect for these parents. Parenting is not an easy task when all life circumstances are in balance, let alone when elements of day-to-day life are a struggle due to unforeseeable circumstances, such as physical health or economic struggles.

We ask a lot from parents in CAMHS: we put them in the 'hot seat', asking them to explain to us the core of their family experiences, what might have gone wrong to bring them to ask someone else for help with their own child. We scrutinise everything that happened during the pregnancy and through each step of their child's life, while looking for clues. Clearly, assessments are conducted with as much compassion, empathy and warmth as possible, although to a parent, the scenario may be experienced as particularly exposing. Parents can show immense strength in making themselves vulnerable by explaining the challenges a child has had to face. Some parents communicate great shame in these situations but remain present and engaged for their child. Using warmth and empathy as a compassionate practitioner can encourage parents to engage with feared experiences such as acknowledging current or historical difficulties. Containing this information in a careful, non-judgemental and accepting manner allows a parent to feel safe and begins the process of providing a nurturing relationship, perhaps also allowing a parent to believe that their child will be safe in therapy. This can be brilliant to witness, as it demonstrates a good degree of emotional courage on the parents' behalf, which allows hope for the therapist that some ingredients for change are already present. Having a compassion-focused approach is particularly important in these cases; we must know that to be truly helpful we must have a full understanding of the child and family circumstance, rather than entirely avoiding subjects that might be difficult for parents. As clinicians facilitating this process, we have a responsibility to use the information wisely and in a way that will provide as positive an outcome for families as possible.

From caring comes courage.

Lao Tzu

Conflict exists in that those who we need to mobilise to support the children are often those who are part of, or maintaining, the problem. There is a range in how amenable families are to hearing such feedback and working with it. Decisions must be made at times as to whether any work with the system is likely to be beneficial or whether intervention ought to be focused on helping the child develop skills to cope, as well as whether it is possible with the system they have. Naturally, this kind of decision is more likely to be made about adolescents rather than children.

Many professions are recognising that patients are becoming 'expert patients' now we are in the internet age. Certainly, several psychiatric diagnoses have developed societal understanding, which is often a reductionist version of symptoms; for example, people may describe their relatives as 'a bit OCD' because they like to keep their space tidy. This trend is reflected in the families of our young people. Some parents begin their CAMHS assessment with a determined belief that their child has a diagnosable condition – that if they keep repeating 'problematic behaviour', fitting the broad and socially understood diagnostic criteria, it will be recognised and labelled. Those lacking the ability to regulate their emotions are considered to have mood swings (surely not in the teenage population, I hear you cry) and therefore the child's behaviour must equate to bipolar disorder. Those who find their child troublesome to parent – 'He won't sit still' – say the reason is that their child has attention deficit hyperactivity disorder (ADHD). It is important to highlight that parental views are considered and respected; where there are features of such conditions present, this will, of course, be acknowledged with the parents. A parent making a suggested diagnosis is never simply assumed to be incorrect. These parents can be understood in many ways. One may be that the parent has been so concerned about their child that they have researched thoroughly and are therefore making an informed contribution. Another may be that the parent presents in such a way because they have tried long and hard to do what is best for their child and struggled to make any progress on their own. This leads to people feeling desperate to be heard and understood when they finally achieve (because it may be an achievement depending on the service) an appointment with a CAMHS professional who will listen. Alternatively, a parent may be locating a child's presentation as something that must be something wrong with them, positioning the child as the problem. A few parents have little awareness of, or struggle with the ability to consider, alternatives other than there being something medically wrong with their child.

On occasions when diagnoses are made, it is important to spend time with parents, giving them permission to recognise any feelings of loss and disappointment they may experience and, in addition, parents frequently appreciate being given permission to need help. Diagnoses can be seen as an official acknowledgement of a child or family's apt and adaptive response to adversity, which can reduce shame for the child and family. Using time with parents to help them cultivate compassion for themselves, both because they deserve it and because they often have very low levels of self-compassion, can be important so they can model it for their youngsters. I'd predict that witnessing true self-compassion in action by the people in your family home ought to be the best way of learning it and believing in it. This, crucially, facilitates parents having a loving, connected presence with their children in the way we try to model in our work with both parties.

A compassionate approach also gives parents permission to parent their children – the responsibility that links to actions. We help parents learn techniques for a compassionate approach to life, helping explore the question 'What can I do today to make tomorrow better for all?' Is that to let a child stay up late because it's easier than a nightly battle or to enforce a boundary to be consistent and predictable for a child? Okay, in this example it may not literally make tomorrow easier, but post-child's resistance, consistent boundaries are always more helpful for all involved.

We often have difficult conversations with parents involving clinical content, such as disclosures of abuse or risk, or content of indicated interventions, such as the need for social workers to be involved or a parenting intervention. Using empathy and compassion, by way of kindness with responsibility, for some of these conversations makes parents feel less blamed and shamed and more open to accepting the situation in discussion. This non-judgemental approach aims to help parents' distress tolerance and models several skills such as perspective taking.

I think it's fair to say that a compassionate approach probably comes fairly naturally to people who have put themselves in a job where they are aiming to help vulnerable people, that is, compassion towards people who we would automatically feel deserve it. However, the crux of real compassion, as reported by the compassionate mind/Compassion Focused Therapy (CFT) movement, is that everyone is deserving of it. This is something that may take a little more work but, whether it is conceptualised as compassion or not, many workers try to think about the shoes that others, in this case parents, may be walking in. We naturally find it easier to have compassion and empathy for things we can understand or can logically explain. In CAMHS there are situations in which parents may be inadvertently damaging their child or neglecting their needs, knowingly or not, and we may find these situations more difficult when our primary role is to advocate for the vulnerable child. I think it would be easy to understand why if therapists feel threatened they can move from utilising a model of psychological distress best treated by compassion in the form of collaboration and mutual learning using guided discovery and a Socratic approach, to adopting a medical model that, in theory, has clearly defined and undisputable pathways. In my experience, this change in thinking is only likely to be noticeable to the therapist and may mean decisions are taken from a different perspective. An example to illustrate this continues from the scenario described previously – a parent is aggressively reporting that they are certain their child has ADHD, but it is clear from other information available that there may be an alternative formulation, such as having heard from the education team that the child has no problems in the school setting. It may be that the child does have ADHD. Either way, it is likely the child would benefit from interventions to make their home environment more manageable. If the parent is unable to think flexibly and becomes aggressive about the need for assessment, it may be that we choose to begin official assessment with an awareness that the child is unlikely to receive the diagnosis. In this scenario, if the parent had a different manner, the decision over initial intervention may be different.

There are times in which CAMHS workers may to struggle to find compassion with some parents, whether this is within their awareness or not. We may be positioning these parents as 'different from us', and perhaps thinking that the parents are unaware of their own contributions to the problem keeps us protected. That way, it wouldn't happen to us; we wouldn't end up in this situation. Perhaps there is protective thinking such as 'I always ask x, y, and z so I would notice' or 'When I have kids I'll not x, y, z' in order that 'I won't be distressed and trying hard to convince a professional to understand my difficulties parenting my child, or pleading for a diagnosis to help the world understand they're not just a naughty child…' Is it possible that fear of sitting in the other chair would make us feel that way? Some of us may have sat in that chair and may judge other parents more harshly for it: 'My [insert name] has real problems if you just listened to yours…' I'd like to think this does not happen much, and these feelings are taken to supervision as a way of managing them responsibly. These reactions are the probable product of hardship that we should empathise with but need to be addressed in order that we use a fully compassionate approach, that is not just being soft, warm and empathetic, but also being assertive to move forward with responsibility and a will to improve situations.

There but for the grace of god go I.

For children

I don't consider myself to have any particular neuro training outwith that of clinical training, but I have gained an understanding from the writings and teachings of those who are experts, such as Bruce Perry, Jonathan Baylin, Daniel Hughes and colleagues to help me learn. From my understanding, for the many young children we see who have had a wide range of adverse early life experiences, biology has worked to protect the child by adapting neural systems to aid survival, but this can have unhelpful lasting effects for the child. Unfortunately, whatever the intensity or duration of the child's adverse experiences, there can be changes in their neurological environment affecting the ability for a child's brain to develop skills central to soothing and nurture and their ability to focus and learn. This often happens in two broad routes: an absence of stimuli needed to encourage growth and development, or a dominant presence of threat.

Where a child may have been neglected through absent or unavailable parents, the impact on a child's development varies depending on the extent of the neglect. It could be as extensive as a lack of basic nutrients to allow a child to thrive and manage interactions with another. Harlow's monkey study (1961) would suggest mammalian contact would be a priority for a child over a meal and the lack of it therefore may be more damaging. A child with these experiences may have learnt helplessness and a total lack of understanding of identity. The alternative end of the scale may be emotional neglect by parents who were present but not available or aware of a child's needs. This usually leads to children not having a chance to learn fine sophisticated skills such as the ability to self-soothe and emotionally regulate. It must be said that in the complex families we work with, these difficulties are often transgenerational, suggesting that parents may not themselves have had the nurturing environment necessary to allow them to learn these skills.

How extensive the results of these adversities are will be shaped by the age and developmental stage of the child. It is generally understood that the younger the child, the more difficulties they may face in the future. Whilst taking a child out of an adverse environment and placing them in safety will be beneficial, it is hard to know how pervasive the impact may be. If a child has been living in an environment that is dominated by threat, their brain makes primitive but sophisticated changes to allow the body to maintain reactions to threat and thus maintain survival. Such changes often leave children in a state of hypervigilance, living in a threat-focused state where survival and safety seeking are central to the child's biology, whether the threat is a current reality or wholly from past experiences. A developing child in an environment of neglect, uncertainty, unavailable parenting or conditional love, intentionally or not, can leave a child in drive mode, constantly striving, acting out to avoid being stuck with their residual feelings.

These are children referred to our service for 'outbursts of anger', 'aggression', 'challenging behaviour', 'requiring assessment for ADHD', 'crippling anxiety' and 'panic attacks'. They are rarely referred for, but often present with, aspects of dissociation. Many of these children lack the ability to emotionally regulate or indeed have found maladaptive means to soothe themselves or avoid feeling. This grows a population of people who self-harm and look to substance or alcohol abuse. Shame is pervasive through this population as a dark and closely guarded emotion. Many children don't have the words to name shame, though they can describe it and display it.

For all of these reasons, the important work of therapists is to help a child to develop skills to self-soothe and find a sense of predictability and safety in their world. Boundaries of therapy help a child develop feelings of safeness and aid their willingness to endure discomfort. We aim to help children learn to nurture their own needs and, through gentle modelling and curiosity, perhaps consider an alternative story to normalise and de-pathologise their experience. We would aim for children to develop some acceptance, self-esteem and self-confidence. This need has been recognised with the influx of mindfulness and CFT. Better minds than mine have explained how to use a compassion-focused approach to work with clients, so I would direct you to the work of authors such as Gilbert, Kolts, Welford and colleagues for the detail, but on reflection, using this approach with children seems effective. Young people have really been able to engage with this approach, particularly because central to CFT is the notion of collaboration and equality; children are already 'controlled by adults' in many arenas of their world and it would be detrimental if this space were another. Young people have responded well to the idea of compassion for the younger version of themselves in particular, but, in addition, in basic chair work, perhaps because some children are less inhibited by the idea of some activities than adults. CFT lends itself well to the adaptions that we would find ourselves making for young people in any other therapeutic approach.

For therapists

One can not reflect in streaming water. Only those who know internal peace can give it to others.

Lao Tzu

Working with this approach is not sustainable without our own self-compassion. Self-care as CAMHS professionals is critical but difficult in a challenging work environment. Self-compassion can be harder for therapists who may be primarily used to focusing on others. We must learn to tone up our own nurture to counterbalance the *strive* or, unfortunately perhaps, the threat mode that many of us can easily begin to work in. To be available to be present for others' suffering, we must be mindful of our own emotional resources and spend the time to maintain them. Training particularly varies in this area; I would consider myself to have had comprehensive training in self-care on my doctoral course, which has been consolidated in qualified practice, but I am still recognising the potential slippage in decision making away from what may be best for me as a practitioner at times. A compassion-focused approach offers guidance by ensuring I take responsibility for taking care of myself and those I work with and helps me have the wisdom to keep checking in on what I'm trying to achieve when making decisions.

As we explain to the parents and children in our service, we must try to do what is going to be genuinely best for us, rather than take the easiest option and perhaps let ourselves off the hook. These scenarios occur multiple times a day:

- Do we stay late to get those notes written up but arrive home later with a clear mind or leave work on time perhaps with an uneasy feeling in the evening and notes to catch up on at the start of a new day?

- Do we book our patients in to the only spare hour we have next week or make them wait for another week to be seen?

Naturally, this will depend on the patient and service demands, but we must always try to remember that this line of work, whilst it can often be a positive and hopeful experience, can also drain us.

It is helpful to plan in slippage for processing time and unplanned duty or crisis work. So, is it better for us to have many people booked in so they are seen sooner or to have the patient wait a little longer and potentially get a more mindful and present therapist? The latter may be a more responsible approach, but there won't ever be a categorical right or wrong answer in these situations, which is the reason workers across the nation are snowed under and burning out. Neither option is ideal as a blanket rule; we need to use self-compassion to choose what is good for us in our own context, rather than what is generally perceived to be the easiest option.

The shame of requesting help

Many of us who are programmed to put our needs behind a list of others' needs may feel it is indulgent, admitting failure or a sign of weakness to request help. Self-compassion is the ideal antidote for our own attitudes in this situation. We must do what we can individually to look after ourselves and tone up our nurture, rather than only be striving to meet targets or working out of threat of breaching waiting lists and such like (see Hacker Hughes *et al.* 2016). We can work to foster a culture in the workplace in which supervision and peer case discussion are available as valuable learning opportunities. These forums are ideal to apply the compassion-focused skills we use in therapy, such as in addressing resistance and blocks to compassion, perspective taking and working with the self-critic to improve our work practices. It is so easy in our current environment to not address these issues. The British Psychological Society (BPS) and

New Savoy Partnership (2015) have recently documented findings of a survey of the wellbeing of mental health workers. This highlighted that 46 per cent of respondents had experienced depression and 50 per cent of respondents felt like they were a failure at work. These figures make grim reading for headlines but allow hope that the BPS will be acting to raise awareness and try to reduce this phenomenon across services.

He who knows others is wise. He who knows himself is enlightened.

Lao Tzu

Conclusion

Through discussing the areas of CAMHS work in which compassion is relevant, I hope it has become clear that a compassionate approach is important for everyone we encounter! It is clear from the growing evidence base that compassion-focused work is developing and moving into services. The approach is filtering out across workplaces, and I hope we can all think about how we tone up our own nurture to help model a compassion-focused approach.

When I originally used the following quotation, I picked it thinking of children, those who I believe in many ways to be the most vulnerable and soft people in the world, in testament to the amazing, resourceful resilience we see in practice. Children demonstrate remarkable signs of hope for the future in circumstances when we could scarcely believe them to have any optimism. I am now including it again because it becomes relevant for any of us who dare to be vulnerable and can find the emotional courage to apply self-compassion to find a way forward.

The softest things in the world overcome the hardest things in the world.

Lao Tzu

References

British Psychological Society and New Savoy Partnership (2015). *Charter for Psychological Wellbeing and Resilience.* Available at www.bps.org.uk/system/files/Public%20files/Comms-media/press_release_and_charter.pdf, accessed on 5 April 2017.

Hacker Hughes, J., Rao, A. S., Dosanjh, N., Cohen-Tovée, E., Clarke, J. and Bhutani, G. (2016). Physician heal thyself (Luke 4:23). *The British Journal of Psychiatry, 209*(6), 447–448.

Harlow, H. F. (1961). The development of affectional patterns in infant monkeys. In B. M. Foss (ed.) *Determinants of Infant Behaviour I.* London/New York: Methuen/Wiley.

Maslow, A. H. (1943). A theory of human motivation. *Psychological Review, 50,* 370–396.

5

Advancing the Philosophy and Science of Caring through Compassion

Mary Prendergast

Director of Nursing, St Patrick's Hospital

My interest for compassionate caring comes from my experience over many years as a nurse, educator and patient advocate. I am privileged and honoured to be part of a service that cares for older people across a variety of settings: services including both medical and orthopaedic rehabilitation, where there are multidisciplinary-focused teams that offer therapeutic inpatient and outpatient facilities in conjunction with day hospital services, residential and respite rotation; and offering advanced memory and cognition assessments with an advanced nurse practitioner and consultant-led teams. I have been a nurse for almost 36 years. I have often contemplated how I could explain to my students what it is like being a patient just for one day, consistently facing the challenges that illness presents – to appreciate how much a smile, a caring touch or a knowing look means to a vulnerable patient. Compassionate interventions cost nothing, just the generosity of spirit that helps us to appreciate the importance of little things given and shared with others in a loving and caring way. Therefore, it is my personal belief that compassion is the true pulse to recovery and the heart of healing. The art of medicine is a collaborative approach, and nurturing compassion fills us with resilience and inspires hope. I can only hope that, in some small way, we touch the lives of our most vulnerable when we reach out in compassion to their situation.

Introducing toolkits to support staff and patient alike will encourage professionals to embed the principles of compassion in their practice. The use of creative tools and concepts provides a mechanism to apply results of appreciative enquiry and revitalises attitudes and approaches to our patients. It enables staff to respond to patients' needs by listening with understanding and appreciating the patient's situation through reflective practice and person-centred care. It is by listening with open ears of the heart that we bring not only our patients, but also our staff together to explore how we can help each other and ourselves to look beyond endeavours to nurturing, for it shapes our responses. Self-care is vital to restoring a sense of joy and igniting a sustained connection, cultivating the light in the heart of each person. This illuminates the qualities they aspire to and work with each day. To do this, we offer retreat days where teams take some time from the workplace to regenerate an attitude of gratitude for all the goodness in their lives and tangibly acknowledge their gifts, talents and reactions to their work. It gives them an opportunity to use their wisdom to analyse what they contribute in service to others. The purpose of the retreats is to gain awareness of self-care, love and acceptance of oneself. This is an important principle in finding strength and resilience – by finding the joy in one's life.

Advocacy and compassion

My interest in patient advocacy and my desire to communicate more effectively about things that matter most to our patients initiated a journey of organisational and personal change to a values-based culture that identified compassion as one of the most significant values.

Leadership is one of the key concepts that drives compassion and triggers an inspired and passionate response to the most intimate care needs. As a healthcare professional, it is a deep privilege to care for those who cannot care for themselves. It is often most humbling to see the desired outcomes being met. To enter the personal space of another so as to facilitate those essential care needs requires a dignified approach and a thoughtful understanding of those being cared for. We need to be decisive, empathic and focused in our approach to caring, identifying the core values of what is important to us in the care-delivery process. Appreciative enquiry is necessary to ensure connection and reflection on practices as holistic caregivers. The power that organisations hold is in the essence of their humanity and the ultimate awareness of compassionate actions offered in the spirit of kindness and hope. This is recognised as a required ingredient to make an organisation's transformational approach truly effective. Fundamentally, transformational leadership emanates for those healthcare professionals with autonomy who create an inspired vision. This leadership approach motivates through influence so others engage in that vision with optimism, confidence and honesty. Where the components of advanced skills, education and knowledge are balanced with compassionate kindness, promoting understanding and commitment among healthcare teams, staff will achieve the right levels of collaboration and flexibility to create profound healing environments.

When there is a greater understanding that moments of healing engagement are important and the structure of the working areas allows time for these moments, outcomes for patients improve. The willing pause to engage with patients and listen attentively to them provides a framework for supportive measures of individualised person-centred caring and comfort. It is my experience that many patient reflection diaries consistently highlight being treated well. Indeed, many patients consider the kindness and compassionate approaches of staff as second only to the competence of their healthcare practitioner. This indicates the importance and significance of compassionate approaches in healthcare as a requirement in the healing process.

On one particular occasion, I remember the wife of a new resident coming through the hospital while she was sad and sobbing. As I rushed to reach my office for a management meeting, I stood for a while to observe this very distressed lady. I approached gently and invited her to sit, held her hand and she cried. There were some affectionate looks but in the greater silence there were only her tears. After some time, I introduced myself and gently prompted a little conversation. I learned that she had looked after her husband with degenerating health and now dementia for ten years. They had no children and were extremely close throughout their marriage. She told me that it broke her heart to let him go into residential care but, with her own health failing and her husband's care needs increasing, she could not cope any more. She advanced from the garden area to the coffee area, and I stayed with her as she reminisced about her life and the joy of knowing the man he was and the life they shared. That evening, I advised the care teams of her distress, which she had not shared with staff. Knowing the complete story enabled them to fully meet the emotional needs of both carer and resident. It gave them a greater empathy, kindness and understanding about the carer's loss in allowing others to care for her husband. I called her the following day to see how she was doing. These were lovely moments of engagement.

She wrote a few months later to say that knowing that her husband was receiving compassionate and competent care was a great source of support to her. The understanding of her situation and the kindness shown to her in the first few weeks of his admission helped her to cope and to come to terms with her husband's illness. This is a very simple account of how healing moments of engagement support compassionate practice.

Most healthcare professionals are in agreement that it is humbling to achieve a greater understanding of the person you are caring for. Person centeredness, advocacy and the caring sciences collectively assist improved organisational practice. This recognises the significance of dignified, respectful and appropriate care needs being met with compassion as being a vital presence that will aid improved organisational practice.

Inspire hope and illuminate a path of awareness

This chapter explores the experience of a value-based system. As discussed so far, change and cultural norms are influenced where compassionate approaches have worked well and where compassion is the fundamental core, supporting resilience and self-care.

As a beginning we have to learn how to offer caring love, forgiveness, compassion and mercy to ourselves before we can offer authentic caring, tenderness, compassion, love and dignity to others.

Dr Jean Watson

The basis for the design of toolkits and training is offered as a mechanism of responding and its significance in measuring care needs and effectiveness. It will seek to outline the view that compassion is an emotional response but one founded on good reason and noble principles that are often innate to us as human beings. This then defines the design and mechanisms of how we care for ourselves and each other.

Compassion is a lived value that is particularly constant and recognisable. It is the unseen kindness of users in the background of all caring interventions, without tagging or naming it. If compassion guides practice then it is part of all aspects of caring: the welcome, the introduction, the assessment, the treatments, the outcomes, the referrals and the discharge. Every action, enquiry and response is part of a compassionate transcendent approach ad infinitum, seen as very much an understood philosophy and over-arching theme through which patient care needs are delivered and met. At every point in the caring chain, compassion breathes clarity, trust, mutual respect and awareness into all actions or words. This chapter is dedicated to the resourceful and generous staff who committed their skills and time in service over the years to the recognition of compassion as a jewel of all qualities in healthcare.

Meaningful values

Within our service, one of the first organisational approaches undertaken was to re-evaluate what philosophy and values would underpin a compassionate way of working in all aspects of the services provided. One of the keys to empowering staff in healthcare today is to re-emphasise the importance of values in guiding practice. Values become meaningful when owned at a personal and professional level so that they become part of the way we work.

The basis of our service experience is that providing opportunities for reflection and self-enquiry will help healthcare practitioners and teams to improve practice. Staff who are able to recognise their own values and discover how their insights can enhance their personal lives will, in turn, revitalise their work. This includes addressing the expectations of others, as well as their personal responses to situations, and in doing this helping to prevent problems of burnout and compassionate fatigue, which creates a healthy working environment. Healthcare organisations and practitioners who use a value-based system benefit at four levels: professional, personal, organisational and educational. The learning experience should be relevant to participants' work and lives, with an emphasis on reflection, action planning and evaluation and a commitment to ongoing learning.

Patient reflections in caring conversations

As a commitment to quality improvement, organisations must gather feedback from patients and their families on an ongoing basis. St Patrick's Hospital Patient Satisfaction Survey (2014) can be used to identify the strengths and weaknesses of an organisation and highlight opportunities for quality improvement initiatives. It is a measure of the patient's perceptions and opinions about the care they receive. It is only by listening to and learning from our patients that we can learn if we have a true appreciation of what represents quality of care in their eyes.

Compassionate thinking – A model for practice
Compassion Footprint

Figure 5.1 Compassion Footprint
Copyright © Mary Prendergast

The Compassion Footprint Model[1] describes capabilities or competencies that can be released naturally from within a person. The compassion footprint for healthcare is used as part of a practical pathway to demonstrate how to deliver person-centred care. It is used as an assessment model for healthcare practice and is concerned with the art of medicine and the application of wisdom in the care and healing process for patients. The footprint represents all the attributes shown in the caring process.

Active restoration of self and of teams – 12 Steps of Restoration[2]
The aim of this programme is to support personal resilience among staff in busy, stressful work environments. Resilience is a complex topic

---

1   The Compassion Footprint Model was created in St Patrick's Hospital, Cashel as part of the Practice Development project by Mary Prendergast.

2   The 12 Steps of Restoration is a mindfulness programme created by Mary Prendergast to help reduce work-related stress. The programme is based on John Kabat Zinn's framework of mindfulness practice.

that is multidimensional. In the field of resilience, there are no quick fixes or instant solutions. It takes commitment and practice for staff to become more resilient. However, for those committed to change and growth, there are approaches to life that if adopted can contribute to an enhanced sense of wellbeing and resilience. This is explored in a coaching framework through the 12 Steps of Restoration. The coaching framework is introduced as follows.

- *Question:* With today's emphasis on quality of service, how can healthcare professionals deliver the best possible care to patients and at the same time feel enriched and supported by their work? How can they thrive and not just survive?

- *Response:* Developing a range of strategies and techniques to tackle stress and build resilience, including relaxation skills, lifestyle management and stress mapping.

- *Action:* The 12 Steps of Restoration addresses an important gap in personal and team development for healthcare facilitated through a one-day programme with a limited group of people. The aim of this one-day programme is to provide relevant learning and skills required by staff to strengthen and sustain them in their role. Upon completion of the programme, participants will be able to develop an internal space by using skills of mindfulness and awareness and developing resources and skills that allow for self-care and care of each other, which creates a flourishing, supportive environment where compassionate frameworks are explored.

On a number of occasions during the programme, staff were very restless about approaching the issue of innate resources and the capacity we all have to sustain and survive in the most difficult of circumstances. One of the most interesting exercises was to have staff explore the mechanism used to reflect on and problem solve how family and friendships sustain us and then to help staff understand the triggers that may cause low mood, rumination and sleep disturbance in stressful situations. During the 12 Steps of Restoration programme facilitators try to link memories with positive experiences and identify resources to keep staff self-autonomous, confident and in control. At one training session, a staff member bravely disclosed her difficulty in building rapport and trusting relationships with colleagues and her experiences of managing this aspect in a professional context. In addition to the helpful and supportive suggestions from colleagues, the programme explored and developed insight into mind/body process, which had a powerful impact upon perceptions of stress and difficulties in the workplace. The programme created awareness of the person-centred care needs of the patients and formed a more integrated approach to the challenges of the working environment and the private and professional challenges one is faced with.

The 12 Steps of Restoration programme is an influential way for improving work performance and helping staff develop their skills. During our workshops, participants work with external energies that affect their wellbeing and capacity to be really present with those who need them. External energies include anger, denial, unmet emotions, family and professional issues.

Natural innate wisdom cues
Tree of Wisdom

Figure 5.2 Tree of Wisdom

The ideology of the tree has great significance in nature and Irish culture. An old Irish saying is: 'Nature's tree is near to earth and near to heaven.' In narrative therapy, we can create stories about trees (us) weathering traumatic, depleting storms where trees lose their leaves and branches but emerge knowing their strength (see Denborough 2008).

The concept of the tree is based on a connection with energy and healing. Just as the tree has deep roots in the earth, an organisation has many skills aligned with knowledge and competency gained in practice at many levels of consciousness. The damaged bark of the tree represents negativity, poor attitude, harsh engagements and abuse of power, which if allowed to develop, will damage any organisation. A tree with a healthy bark indicates positivity and authenticity.

We can choose to be positive, to be the best we can be in every moment. We can change environments into healing places by being aware. There is a gentleness and kindness in environments where appreciation exists. By adapting values of humility and humanity from the heart, we create a positive flourishing energy.

The five branches represent five graces of human interaction: connection, reflection, power, love and service, which are all used in caring conversations, reflective practice and action learning.

Just like us, a tree can weather a storm because it has innate qualities to do so. Human beings also have these qualities. With every storm, we learn to adapt more and are renewed just like the leaves of the tree.

Engaging with competence
Healing Moments of Engagement

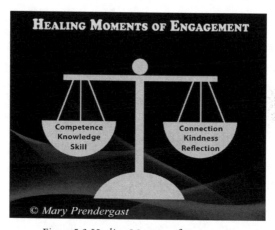

Figure 5.3 Healing Moments of Engagement

Learning how to engage with patients is critical. An understanding of the connection while delivering care is important. Care delivery, which can often be quite intimate, is a precious space that is privileged – a place of invitation for the caregiver. Both patient and carer often connect with each other in the most heartfelt way.

Care is given and received in a space of gentleness, deep trust, compassion and respect. There are values identified with special, intimate, caring experiences where power, love, competence and spirituality are entwined as one. How often do we stop to think about the connection we make? It is an honour and privilege to step into those moments of healing engagement. The art of healing is nurtured through connection and love.

I visited a unit where a patient had been admitted some weeks previously. Staff had tried everything to connect with him. They were slowly building real trust and connection. However, they felt this patient's great sadness about his illness and frailty after his life-changing event of complicated, advanced, cerebral vascular dementia. So the team decided to try every professional approach available to restore this man's self-esteem. In the following days, I had occasion to speak to his son. He was upset at his father's sadness and disinterest in life, and I took time to chat with him about his father's life and loves. His father was a primary schoolteacher who loved sport, children and reading. After further exploring, I discovered that his father wrote poetry on occasion. Poetry at its best can cure the saddest heart and take us all to a place of joy and healing. We arranged for his son and family to read some poetry each evening to his father. I suggested that when his father could speak the son could sit and tape him reading his own poetry and anything new he would like to voice and to have typed up. By finding a meaning and purpose in his life, he regained a sense of autonomy and control.

After trial and error, this man found his creativity again – not with the same independence but with a different interdependency that allowed his expression. Healing is evident when engagement is real and tangible. Healing moments of engagement occur where competence, skills and knowledge are balanced by the kindness, connection and reflection of what matters most to our patients.

Conscious caring – creating peaceful environments with collaboration and leadership

The Conscious Caring Programme, which I developed within St Patrick's Hospital and now train others in, is divided into three study elements, namely: Creating Peaceful Working Environments, Collaboration in Healthcare Environments and Leadership in Healthcare. Compassionate leadership and conscious caring in healthcare assist mechanisms of ensuring public confidence in the quality and safety of care, treatment and services. This process gives our patients confidence through ensuring consistently high standards in care and making a strong statement about the organisation's efforts to provide the highest quality service. The Compassionate Leadership Conscious Caring in Healthcare programme provides the knowledge and competence to follow best practice in terms of person-centred care. Here are eight critical questions that support practitioners to create a supportive environment where compassionate leadership and conscious caring can flourish:

- What is compassion and how do we teach compassion?

- What are the practical things practitioners can do?

- How do we care for our patients in a more conscious-caring way through compassionate approaches?

- How do we demonstrate compassionate leadership in our practice?

- How does this practice influence patient care?

- What are the values that influence our practice?

- What is mindful restoration of body, mind and spirit?

- Are there sanctuaries where mindfulness is explored?

Influences in practice

Thoughts are like building bricks of life: everything begins with a thought. When we add enthusiasm to thoughts of inspiration, we find ways to influence with ease and gentleness. Every tower starts in conscious thought among the breezy folds of imagination. It is then grounded by the architects and engineers that expand our horizons and create the picture to achieve the desired outcomes. We must fuel our compassionate approaches to care with aspiration and confidence, aiming not just for the set standard as a benchmark, but also to stretch ourselves and the organisation beyond comfort zones to a conscious awareness at a higher level. Here the connection between the patient and the carer's incredible human spirit will enable the intentions to start the creation process of something radiant and reflective. Kindness melts barriers of coldness and we move forward with a warm heart. This empowers us to take on the challenges ahead. And then we do not feel isolated – these are the willing attributes useful in co-creating nurture, synchronicity, warmth and flow.

Cooperation is fuelled by using the gifts, interests and talents of individuals on staff teams. It eliminates power struggles, conflict and competition. Such cooperation promotes harmony and togetherness and brings out the best in each one. The process of finding and exploring how we can mutually assist each other in a partnership process brings everyone together. The attitude of sharing compassion benefits all staff and patients alike, endeavouring to create happiness in the working environments. Happiness in a workplace is important, as it enhances positive ways of achieving outcomes. Wellbeing is intrinsically liked with performance research. Findings suggest autonomy, meaning and good relationships are not only valuable assets in the workplace, but also accomplishments in our private lives (Seligman 2011). In some models, such as Seligman's PERMA model (2011), key areas that feed into life satisfaction have been named as positive emotion, engagement, meaning and purpose. So, it is reasonable to present a case where staff and patients are treated in the same vein in accordance with an organisational philosophy and set of values that place compassion at the organisation's core. There is a responsibility for leaders to be part of a partnership, where staff feel sufficiently content, cared for and stretched in a developmental way to achieve success.

> *Let us be grateful to people who make us happy and appreciate us; they are the charming gardeners who make our souls blossom.*
>
> *Marcel Proust*

This question remains: 'How do these concepts influence compassionate practice?'

The models act as awareness indicators where staff can use many models to find deeper meaning and purpose in their work. The concepts ignite a potential to explore creatively new ideas relative to compassionate practice. They are a creative reminder of how we need to be empowered. As a professional, and whole person, we need to channel the face of understanding and judgement in a trusting and reactive way to help our staff to function in a safer, healthier and happier way and to use their discernment to respond with intuition to situations as they unfold. Creativity is an energy of adventure and change. It heralds new ideas and inspiration. Compassion is an expression and commitment in the working environment. It is a key in relationships or projects. It is a journey toward a vision of compassion in action, for nothing is more powerful than a focused energetic awareness. Where clarity rests, strength lies in decisions to respond with maturity. This brings fulfilment and satisfaction to the team and a unity that attracts success.

Appreciative enquiry

As organisations focus on values, there is a sense that we are prioritising patient-centred care, and everything else relevant will align itself around these values. There is a need to determine the best way of delivering services with consideration of one's needs and honesty around time commitments, goals, hopes and aspirations. There are many occasions when organisations should ask 'How can I get that one per cent closer to the best possible outcome?' Having resourcefully navigated waters and put the changes in place, this should feel comfortable, natural and effective for all. Committed staff will not harbour failures but will see positives in the process. Successful or not, where useful elements are found to foster compassion in organisations, we should adapt them. The gratitude for what is achieved is important. We all want to feel like winners and not to be diminished by failures. We must have commitment as a team not to allow negativity or objections to hold the power in our working projects. We should recognise the efforts of good people who make a difference to our services and our patients. In doing so, we understand the risks but also focus on the rewards, learn from mistakes and avoid linear thinking. Teams move on with the planned focus of seeking improvements and securing better patient outcomes. Connection and reflection is always the key to quality focus. The question 'What would I do differently next time?' should remain part of the communication process with patients and teams.

The phrase 'No chastising or blaming – just engaging' always has a very powerful confidence-boosting effect. My team found that benchmarking practices against others yielded benefits in quality terms. However, supporting the self-worth and vitality of the team produces enormous results in influencing and problem solving. Gold medals are won in the game of life through the legacy of how we treat and care for others. We can forgive ourselves for being less brilliant than others and we can all carry out acts of kindness that make a great difference. It is a privilege to be a healthcare professional where compassionate caring is shown in words and deeds and where we truly value humanity.

Conclusion

In reality, whatever mechanism, toolkit or approach is perceived by the organisation as most favourable to advance compassionate practice, the philosophy of its generic style must be a lived value. As Nelson Mandela said, 'May your choices reflect your hopes and not your fears.' We need to nurture staff so that they self-care and do not develop symptoms of compassion fatigue, burnout and stress. Authentic compassionate care promotes self-empowering models that reflect how care is provided. Compassion sits in the heart and is the inspiration in every footprint at the patient's bedside. It should be the norm and not the exception so that compassionate care is a commitment to a way of working. Thich Nhat Hanh (Vietnamese Buddhist monk and peace activist) wrote 'when you care for someone, the best thing you can offer them is your presence'. Awareness of one another is necessary to treat others in a way that you would like to be treated yourself. Ask only of others what you would be willing to give yourself. In difficult moments, it is necessary to reflect on the source of life and living. We should take nothing for granted in our professional and private lives. We need to breathe deeply, look up and engage with our eyes, love with our heart, forgive easier and move on gracefully.

References

Denborough, D. (2008). *Collective Narrative Practice: Responding to Individuals, Groups, and Communities who have Experienced Trauma*. Adelaide: Dulwich Centre Publications.

Nhat Hanh, T. (2006) *Understanding Our Mind: Fifty Verses on Buddhist Psychology*. Parallax Press, California.

Seligman, M. (2011). *Flourish: A Visionary New Understanding of Happiness and Well-being*. New York: Free Press.

St Patrick's Hospital Patient Satisfaction Survey (2014). *Annual Review of St Patrick's Mental Health Services Outcomes*. Available at: www.stpatricks.ie/sites/default/files/Outcomes%20Report%202014.pdf, accessed on 5 April 2017.

6

Compassionate Practice Transforming Lives

Edith Macintosh

Rehabilitation Consultant and Occupational Therapist

As the rehabilitation consultant for the Care Inspectorate, the scrutiny and improvement body for care services in Scotland, I have the privilege of thinking about and enabling improvement in the social care sector every day. In my role, I attempt to find out what matters to people, those being cared for and the staff who do the caring, and together we discover possible solutions to any challenges that prevent hopes, dreams and ambitions being fulfilled, no matter how big or how small. Working with many different partners, I engage in effective conversations about what needs to improve and how we can do that well, and importantly, in a way that lasts.

In this chapter, I am going to share some of my thoughts on compassion, my personal experience of sharing compassion, how I have been influenced and how this has shaped my approach to others in and out of work over the past years.

Some of what I do in my work is about influencing health and social care policy and promoting good practice in the care sector locally, nationally and internationally. Working with other organisations, I also develop educational solutions for the care sector across Scotland to help them build capacity and capability within the workforce and ultimately improve the quality of care people receive. What motivates me to have a passion for this work is the desire to help people sustain their existence in a way that gives them meaning and purpose in their lives, whatever their situation and for as long as they live. Compassion for me is about building hope in people or in situations.

I believe if we have hope and, quite simply, a reason to get up each morning, this helps builds resilience to live life well despite illness or disability.

We all need a goal in life, something to aim for that is driven by what matters and motivates us. Some of us will be more aware of what matters and motivates us than others, but it's still true! If we lose our focus and drive, it can be difficult to be hopeful that good things are just around the corner and bounce back if we have hard times.

Participation in life is crucial. It strengthens our sense of citizenship – that feeling of belonging that I believe is an inherent need in us all – and it helps us to be part of society and all that brings in terms of roles, choices and rights and having our contribution recognised and valued. In the social care sector across Scotland, I witness people having that compassionate heart response; they recognise that *need* when someone has lost their focus and give of themselves, in whatever way, to make life worth living again and again for those who need their support. A true compassionate response from a caring community.

In preparation for writing this chapter, I asked friends and colleagues: 'When I say the word compassion, what do you feel and what does that mean to you?' A whole variety of answers came back, from charity work where people are responding to national disasters and alleviating human suffering on a large scale to having a depth of connection with someone that reassures, brings confidence and lets them know someone is walking that hard road with them. Some said it is a heart response built on knowing someone and some a spontaneous gut response – there is no right or wrong, is there? Everyone's experience of giving and receiving compassion will be a bit different and the emotional basis for that experience will also be different. Compassion is said, by some, to be the supreme human virtue. The Dalai Lama once said 'compassion is a necessity not a luxury' (Lama and Cutler 1998), which for me sounds true and, on reflection, I wonder if that sounds a bit like 'love' or 'love in action'. I would suggest we all need to be loved and to give love. I wouldn't like to live in a world without love and compassion!

When I think about my years working as an occupational therapist, I can remember particular occasions where I felt a stronger sense of compassion for particular patients. That strong, heartfelt longing to be able to do miracles and change things for the better! Where your heart almost breaks for people and situations, and you often feel a sense of helplessness as part of the compassionate response.

When I was very young, a close member of my family was blessed with a beautiful little girl. He and his wife had waited many years for this gift of life. She was adorable; everyone loved little Karen. When Karen was six months old, she died; she had cancer. No one could believe it had happened. Her parents were, of course, heartbroken for the little girl they had waited so long for, but they were so courageous with a strong faith to get them through the grief they were experiencing. I think I was only about 11 years old when this happened but I can still remember the deep sadness I felt not just about Karen's death but also for her parents and the huge chasm she had left in their lives and their hearts. I felt quite distraught about the fact that I couldn't make it better. I couldn't bring Karen back for them. This may have been one of the first times I felt such a strong response to the suffering and sadness of others.

I would describe compassion for me as a clinician as particularly feeling the distress and sadness of patients, as a result of experiencing unexpected and devastating illness. One of my patients was a middle-aged, fit gentleman who was in Scotland on holiday from Holland when he had a massive stroke. He had no health issues prior to this, enjoyed working out and loved his job as a long-distance lorry driver. In an instant, his life changed; he was completely dependent on others and was filled with dread for the future, instead of hope. He was anxious that he would not be able to work or even look after himself again and was quite depressed. I remember so clearly, early in his rehabilitation, I was working with him in order to regain some function in his right arm. He was really down and I wanted to try to take away his sadness and his suffering. As the session moved on, we spoke together about hopes for the future and what he wanted to be able to do, trying to find the key that would open that door to hope. The session came to an end and there had been little change in him. However, when I went back to see him later in the day, I found quite a different man! His mood had lifted and some function had returned to his arm and hand. He thought I was a miracle worker! I certainly wasn't, but I often wonder if anything changed physiologically as a result of sharing compassion and helping him to see a purpose for his life and hope for a future. That day, his healing began and he eventually returned to an independent and fulfilling life.

In recent years, I have been a volunteer for a charity supporting people living with HIV and Hepatitis C. I became a *buddy* for a young woman who had dealt with many personal and family challenges in her life over her 40 odd years and, as a result, had turned to drugs and alcohol to help her through. We became friends. Initially, I had a real need to try to turn her life around, to save her from herself. After spending many hours talking together, I realised her need in life was to be loved and accepted for the person she was. She was more aware than anyone of the harsh reality of what she described as her failings and bad decisions in life and how these had affected her health and wellbeing, often bringing her to the brink of death. The compassion she looked for was one that could help her to remain herself, the kind of compassion that would keep her identity intact. She liked nothing more than going shopping for CDs of the music she enjoyed or meeting for coffee or lunch and talking about what she hoped to do one day, finding out about my life and hearing about my family. She told me she really looked forward to getting together. Often I came away from these times we spent chatting and drinking numerous mugs of coffee feeling more cared for than I had cared for her! I believe we practised and shared compassion during these times.

I often wonder why I felt such compassion for the people in these two stories; was it because I felt a sense of hopelessness and wanted to bring hope back? I wanted a bright future for them where all their ambitions could be fulfilled. Was it because I felt a particular connection with these people that was a heart response, not just clinical or superficial in any way? Was it because of the way they responded to me, trusting me and knowing I had their best interests at heart? Probably all of these and more.

Providing essential care is so important for those who are physically and cognitively more vulnerable. It is necessary to have food and something to drink and to be clean and suitably dressed; for some, medication and specifics such as wound care will be crucial to living well. However, that without compassion is empty. It is going through the motions with no relationship or real desire to make life better for someone or respect their rights, dignity and choices. This seems to me to be more of an existence rather than living, and it sounds as if there is not a lot of hope. Being compassionate is essential to improving people's experience of care in its fullest form. Compassion is included in the principles for the newly reviewed National Care Standards for Scotland. There is an expectation, and rightly so, that care is provided by a workforce that understands and is sensitive to the needs and wishes of people who they offer support to. The care should be warm, nurturing and supportive at all times – people should have a real desire to help. In order to do that well, you have to really know who someone is – their likes and dislikes, what their needs are, what motivates them, what participation means to them and which people are important to their lives, amongst many other things.

One of the pieces of work I was involved in, an initiative called Make Every Moment Count (Care Inspectorate 2013), helps people to do that, and in fact could be called a tool to aid a compassionate approach.

Make Every Moment Count is a simple guide for care staff, with prompts to support them to enable those they care for to enjoy and take part in everyday life. It was created with input from a group of care staff and other professionals from across health and social care. The care staff said they felt in the most part that they were good at the hands-on caring tasks. However, they also said there was a real need to be reminded of a crucial element of the caring process, which was the importance of having high-quality interactions in order to give the best care experience and achieve good personal outcomes for people. The quality of our interactions with other people can produce a positive or negative impact. Every interaction that takes place in whatever situation is an important one and the approach we take when we interact with others has a significant impact on someone's life for good or bad. Interactions take place during all activities we do, whether that's helping someone to get washed or dressed, giving someone a cup of tea or making eye contact as you pass by a room. You can have a significant impact on a person's quality and enjoyment of life, and indeed their resilience to cope with any of the challenges life may bring, through the quality of an interaction. If our interactions come from the basis of compassion with a true desire to make life better for people, no matter what stage in life they are at, that is powerful and can actually be transformational for everyone involved. I have seen both negative and positive interactions and the results of these. I know of situations where positive interactions have enabled people to reignite a passion and interest they had in the past or be more independent in their daily life. Quality interactions, in some cases, have helped people to reconnect with their local community and be part of society again. I know of carers who have stayed with someone during their last few hours of life, when they should have been home with their family, because they knew it would make a difference to that person to be there until the end due to their special connection. I have witnessed the difference that sitting with someone in companionable silence and living in the moment together has made. All of these are compassionate interactions of a quality that impacted upon people's ability to enjoy life right to the end.

What about the impact on the person who has cared in this compassionate way? In my experience, it can bring a whole host of feelings and emotions. The person may feel a real sense of fulfilment and satisfaction that they have served someone well and often get comfort themselves. It can be quite a strong emotional experience for people if their act of compassion has an unexpected impact, such as someone interacting when they normally would not or enabling someone to have a good end-of-life experience. People often feel good because they have made a positive difference to an individual's life or a situation, for a moment or for longer, by acting on the strong sense of compassion they felt.

Although it has a 'doing' component, compassion is absolutely an emotional or gut response to a person or situation. There are so many good examples of this – role models who have influenced me, helped me to grow and know how to be compassionate to others. In the Bible, stories are told of God's compassion for all the people, even the guilty thief who was dying beside him on a cross. There's Mother Teresa who gave her life to help others who were less fortunate, one of her famous quotes is 'Give, but give until it hurts' (González-Balado 1998). Recently I read the book *Being Mortal* by Atul Gawande (2014), where he writes wonderfully and inspirationally about our crime of medicalising ageing, frailty and ultimately death. He suggests it has become just another thing to try to fix when instead health and social care professionals, and society as a whole, should be making it possible for people to enjoy life to the full and still experience what matters to them.

Gawande says:

> All we ask is to be allowed to be the writers of our own story. That story is ever changing. Over the course of our lives, we may encounter unimaginable difficulties. Our concerns and desires may shift. But whatever happens, we want to retain the freedom to shape our lives in ways consistent with our character and loyalties. (2004, p.42)

I have met so many people, particularly in the care sector, who, despite their age and frailty, can and want to contribute to society, have fun and enjoy life. I recently met a lady with dementia living in a care home who adapted the story of 'Goldilocks and the Three Bears' to write a pantomime that was performed by some residents in the care home, all of whom had dementia, the oldest being 101. The impact of that was huge in terms of quality of life. They spoke about all the fun they had rehearsing, meeting new people, building friendships and having a reason to get up each day.

There's been a growing interest over the last few years in promoting physical activity in the care sector in Scotland, and I am fortunate to be involved in a programme of work that supports that. One aspect of that is to make it possible for older people in care homes to get involved in various sports. One of these sports is swimming and in several areas in Scotland people and organisations have worked together to run projects to make this possible and show others that it can be done. The result of this has been that some people have begun to swim again after 30 years, some have tried something new and loved it, people have made new friendships and rekindled old ones and one or two now go for swimming sessions with swim instructors and visit the local pool that they used to go to many years ago. The care home residents had many positive comments to give such as: 'I feel free again' and 'I feel young again'. Just last month I attended a games challenge for care home residents in a local sports hall. There were over 100 residents there, the oldest being 96. They clearly had a great day and were very competitive. I had the honour of presenting some medals and certificates at the end of the event and one of the recipients started to cry, unable to believe she was getting an award. She was overwhelmed, as she felt she had really lived life that day.

I have two little granddaughters. Millie is just over two years old and Jolie is almost seven months; they are cousins. They love each other very much. Millie is a very energetic girl. She is always on the go and can be over enthusiastic when it comes to personal contact with people! I wondered what she would be like with Jolie when she came along. Initially, the whole family were rather nervous when Millie was around Jolie, imagining that she may unwittingly squeeze Jolie to death! However, very interestingly, even at such a young age, Millie was able to distinguish between those who require a gentler approach. She is so loving and caring and has never once delivered a crushing cuddle or knocked into Jolie with anything as she dashes about. As young as she is, her response is compassionate towards her little cousin; she wants to care for her and make sure she has everything she needs to make her happy. What a lovely example right in front of my eyes.

Millie's nannie was in her 80s when Millie came on the scene. Millie recognised right away there was something different about Nannie. She wasn't the cuddliest of little girls and certainly was not generous with her kisses. However, right away, when she was with Nannie she was different. She would shower her with unexpected hugs and kisses and crawl up on her knee, being very happy to sit there and cuddle her. It was always Nannie's hand she wanted to hold. As you can imagine, Nannie loved her and all the attention she got from Millie; it always made such a difference to her day when Millie was around. A compassionate human response to the more vulnerable in society can happen at a very early age it seems. Does that mean compassion is a part of us and we are born with it?

Compassion may not always be comfortable or for comfort. Sometimes being compassionate does mean having hard conversations. This is hard for the person on the receiving end of this kind of compassion but also for the giver! I have experienced this while helping people to make heart-wrenching life-and-death choices as people near the end of their life, when trying to inspire people to realise their potential despite illness and disability, while encouraging independence when there is no confidence or obvious ability there and the frustrations and hopelessness that can bring. It can sometimes be a delicate balance. What people experience in their lives is unique to them and very individual, as is their response to that. One thing I have learnt is that in order to really help people find their way, you have to be compassionate in a way that fits with their individuality, especially if it is a hard conversation. Compassion is an emotional response but the practical outworking and refining of that may need to be practised. I think I have got better at it over time with life experience. This component of compassion, I feel, is a skill and it may take time to develop.

I've learnt a lot, while training as an occupational therapist and working in health and social care over many years, about medical and psychological ways to help people, ways to adapt the environment and emotional strategies that can be put in place to make life better. I didn't learn about compassion at university and I don't remember people talking a lot about it, and yet look at the difference it makes. In monetary terms, it costs us nothing, and I believe the impact in many situations can be huge and long lasting!

Through writing this chapter, I have reflected on compassion and have drawn a few conclusions that you may or may not agree with!

- We will all need compassion at some time in our life.

- We all have compassion we can give to another person or situation if we choose to.

- Compassion can be shared between people.

- We may feel more compassionate towards certain people or situations or at different times.

- We may find that something stimulates a sudden compassionate response.

- Being compassionate takes time and energy and requires quality human interactions and relationships in order to be most effective.

- We need a compassionate heart and approach to care for people well.

- Compassion can be in the form of 'tough love' when, in order to help others to have hope and be more resilient, we offer challenge.

- Compassion is part of us but we can nurture compassion and develop skills in order to support people more effectively.

- Compassion can be transformational if we let it!

Further information

You can find out more about Make Every Moment Count at: www. careinspectorate.com/index.php/care-news-online/9-professional/ 2736-make-every-moment-count.

References

Care Inspectorate (2013). *Make Every Moment Count. A Guide for Everyday Living*. Dundee: Care Inspectorate.

Gawande, A. (2014). *Being Mortal*. London: Profile Books Ltd.

González-Balado, J. L. (1998). *One Heart Full of Love: Mother Teresa*. Cincinnati, OH: St. Anthony Messenger Press.

Lama, D. and Cutler, H. C. (1998). *The Art of Happiness: A Handbook for Living*. New York: Riverhead Books.

PART THREE

Compassionately Nurturing the Personal and Professional Self

Nestled in that place where feelings and thoughts are one. That place of early experience where we emerge into the world and begin our own journey of sense-making. Where we require the care of an 'other' to survive, where abandonment would mean death and where, if we are fortunate enough, we are bathed in another's love and care that holds us through the most terrifying moments.

Jenny Shuttleworth Davies

7

My Self-Compassion Journey

FROM STRIVING TO SHARING SATISFACTION

Dr Sarah Lawson

Clinical and Coaching Psychologist

Three years ago, I made the decision to change the way I work as a psychologist. In the summer of 2013, having spent ten years studying and training towards my career in clinical psychology, I found myself at a crossroads in my life and questioning the direction I was going next. I became aware that I was headed in the direction of 'burnout', interestingly an area that was central to my doctoral thesis. The passion that had initially attracted me to working in the field of psychology was overshadowed by exhaustion. I felt drained from carrying the weight and responsibility of my clients' problems and disconnected to those closest to me, and there was simply not enough of me left to give. I seriously began to question whether clinical psychology was still the right profession for me.

When I first came across coaching psychology, it had a massive impact on my life, almost immediately. Feeling fatigued from my work, I thought signing up for a two-day coaching course might help as a way of learning and adding different skills to my toolset, as well as offering a change of pace from the levels of distress I was often used to working with.

I was aware that coaching was about supporting clients to make positive changes and promoting psychological wellbeing, but I hadn't considered the personal impact it might also have. As it happened, the course was much more of an experiential workshop than didactic training. It uncovered for me that I was giving too much, trying to get everything right, to fix, as well as a lot of self-critical talk and shame, the list could go on. I was certainly not showing myself compassion.

Further training and experiencing my own coaching led to a breakthrough, and I took a leap into coaching psychology. Coaching has given me a new perspective and a new way of working psychologically, as well as opening the door to a more compassionate way of working with others and towards myself. It has reignited the enthusiasm I once had for working as a psychologist.

As my journey into coaching has developed, I believe that compassion is a vital underpinning to coaching. Engaging in the coaching process, practices and activities from a position of compassion, both as a coach and coachee, have certainly helped me become happier and more fulfilled both personally and professionally.

This chapter will focus on self-compassion in the context of coaching psychology and my individual experience of how coaching has, for me, become a more compassionate way to practise psychology. Similarities and distinctions between coaching and clinical psychology will also be explored. This is by no means meant to highlight one approach as superior, yet I hope it will enable the reader to gain an understanding of coaching and insight into my own experiences of working in both fields. I will also discuss my work with a client, Tina (a pseudonym), and how using compassion in coaching supported her in all aspects of her life. Finally, I will conclude with some reflections and observations.

Burnout and compassion fatigue

Like many helping practitioners, I was motivated to become a psychologist through a desire to care for others and help alleviate their distress. My own personal experiences allowed me to bring a deeper understanding, as well as mastering good therapeutic skills such as careful listening, being empathic and holding a space for my clients. Yet, as I experienced first-hand, there is a cost to caring. Research has highlighted that professionals who listen to clients' stories of fear, pain and suffering may feel similar fear, pain and suffering because they care (Figley 1995). Indirect exposure to client trauma has been shown to have a negative impact on the wellbeing of professionals, putting them at risk of significant cognitive, behavioural and emotional changes (Sabin-Farrell and Turpin 2003).

Empathy is seen as being crucial to working with client distress and trauma, yet it has also been identified as a risk factor in developing compassion fatigue (also referred to as burnout/secondary traumatic stress). Professionals who are most empathic and sensitive tend to be the most at risk, since they feel the pain of their clients most deeply. The therapist's assets, such as empathy, which is a vital tool for the therapy, may go too far and can come at a cost to the therapist.

Aware of the symptoms I was experiencing, yet unsure of how to alleviate them most effectively, it was my own experience of burnout that motivated me to explore coaching. At the time, I believed that having a change of pace and working with less distressed clients would help me. I realise now that experiencing my own personal coaching and the experience of coaching others was my first real experience of and journey to self-compassion.

I was aware of the importance of holding a space and providing empathy for my clients, yet despite this knowledge, I hadn't considered compassion towards myself. I looked after myself in the best way I knew how, mostly in the physical form: exercising, sleeping and eating relatively well. Whilst these have shown to improve both mental and physical energy levels, I still had the thoughts and emotions to deal with. Working with pain, day after day, is painful.

Exploring compassion

In the past decade, there has been growing research and interest in utilising Buddhist concepts for psychological interventions, including compassion. Compassion involves being open and sensitive to suffering, with the desire to alleviate this. Self-compassion refers to directing this towards the self. Self-compassion is conceptualised by Neff (2003) as self-kindness rather than self-criticism; common humanity rather than isolation; and mindfulness rather than over-identification with feelings. These components combine and interact to create a self-compassionate frame of mind.

Experiencing my own coaching opened the door of compassion for me. With help from my coach, Marie, I was able to quieten my inner critic and hear more clearly the kind and compassionate part of myself. I discovered that self-compassion provides a way to fill up our internal reserves, so we have more to give to those who need us, a way of emotionally recharging our batteries. I like the example of it being like the safety information on an aeroplane, explaining that you have to fit your own oxygen mask before helping others. Self-compassion is a reminder that you have to care about yourself before you can really care about other people.

Self-compassion has been identified as a source of eudaimonic happiness (Ryan and Deci 2001). While the hedonic approach seeks to improve short-term happiness, pursuing pleasure and avoiding pain, eudaimonic happiness involves sustaining wellbeing, finding purpose and meaning in one's life. Equally, self-compassion is not about avoiding pain, but rather embracing it with kindness, creating a sense of wellbeing that is rooted in the experience of being fully human. In this way, it is strongly paralleled with many approaches and styles of coaching and certainly the way I have learnt and come to practise coaching is through a compassion-focused approach. Coaching psychology has its grounding in humanistic psychology, an emphasis on the fully functioning person (Rogers 1961), the study of healthy personality (Maslow 1968), self-actualisation and striving to reach one's full potential.

Coaching psychology

Psychology has traditionally, regardless of preferred theoretical orientation, focused on ameliorating distress and repairing dysfunction. Where clinical and counselling psychologists tend to work with clients who are distressed, coaching psychologists work with well-functioning clients to help them to reach their personal and work goals, utilising a wide range of theoretic perspectives. Coaching psychology is defined as 'enhancing well-being and performance in personal life and work domains' (Palmer and Whybrow 2005, p.7), advocating that the remit of the coaching psychologist lies at the more positive end of human functioning.

Fix vs. create

The way most people come into coaching sets it apart from typical therapeutic relationships. Most people in the UK access psychological services through the National Health Service (NHS) where often a label or diagnosis is given before 'treatment'. Clients come with a presenting 'problem', either that they want the therapist to solve or because someone else has sent them. There is an assumption before the therapeutic relationship has begun of something 'broken' needing to be 'fixed'.

The dynamic of the coaching relationship differs from the overtly hierarchical relationship associated with clinical or counselling work. The coaching relationship is collaborative, coming together as two equals. The relationship is mutually designed and both the coach and client are equally involved in making it work. The emphasis is on a non-directional, ask-not-tell approach (Whitmore 1992), with the onus on the client, who is whole, resourceful and complete – not someone who is broken and needs to be fixed! There is a shared humanity: we all make mistakes, we are not perfect and we take responsibility for our own actions and growth.

There is an impetus on promoting psychological wellbeing and the focus is on the client's strengths and possibilities, rather than a particular 'problem'. Whilst the client's expectation for change in therapy is generally from high dissatisfaction to reasonable satisfaction, coaching takes people from relative satisfaction to a much higher level of satisfaction.

Why do people need a coach?

People often come to coaching because they are feeling stuck and they want something to change. More often than not, they have tried to make changes themselves and perceived themselves to have failed, or they are struggling to get started, usually due to an underlying fear of failure (e.g. a fear of not being good enough, a fear of not fitting in, a fear of not being loveable).

Clients who come for coaching often engage in excessive self-monitoring and self-criticism and often lack self-confidence. Excessive self-criticism is common to a wide range of performance and wellbeing issues and can disrupt improving and learning new skills. If people continually negatively monitor their performance then their behaviour becomes disrupted, old patterns are repeated and they don't move forward or make changes.

Making progress in their lives involves people getting in touch with their own difficulties and taking steps to alleviate and prevent them from continuing in the future. A powerful way to do this is to challenge our self-critical voice, acknowledging this and adopting a compassionate voice. Using compassion in coaching helps clients to think and grow into more of the person they want to be. It provides clients with an alternative framework for thinking about their problems, situation and path forward. Self-compassion allows us to acknowledge areas of personal weakness by recognising that imperfection is part of the shared human experience; no one is 'perfect'. We can then work on improving ourselves, not because we're unacceptable as we are, but because we want to thrive and be happy. Increasingly, the research is suggesting that self-compassion is an approach that enables people to suffer less whilst also helping them to thrive. Coaching and compassion help clients reduce their inner critic, talk with themselves in a more accepting and understanding voice and change the way they think, feel and behave.

Case example

One of my very first coaching clients, Tina (a pseudonym), came to coaching because she wanted to improve her work/life balance. She felt that she was never giving enough to either. Tina had a strong inner critical voice and believed that she needed this to help keep her focus and work hard. As we worked together, we uncovered her internal critic was 'so loud (she) could hardly hear herself think'. She believed she needed to stay longer hours than her colleagues at work, as this showed her commitment to her job. She felt anxious most of the time, and despite having a successful career, felt she wasn't good enough at her job. Tina was a high achiever and had already achieved a first-class honours in her degree and a Master's in business. Her belief was that she 'couldn't let herself off the hook' and 'constantly felt she had to keep herself in check'. For her, this way of being had helped her achieve a number of great things in her life. Like most high-achieving people, she was very hard on herself and felt like a failure unless she succeeded. More often than not, she achieved what she set out to but with detriment to other areas of her life. She was becoming aware that it was impacting upon her relationship with her husband and young son and her physical health, as well her relationship with herself. Her internal critic would say 'You should be able to do all of this... you aren't a quitter', 'You need to work harder' and 'If things aren't right, you aren't doing a good enough job.' Listening to the inner critical voice had, in the past, worked as a motivator for her. Tina wanted to be proud of her achievements and for others to be proud of her too, yet she believed the only way she could reach her goals was through intense pressure and constant self-criticism.

I have discussed Tina's experiences as an example here, yet I'm sure we can all relate to some of them. This is a way many of us go about motivating ourselves – telling ourselves that we 'should try harder', 'failure isn't an option' and 'we mustn't let others down'. To some extent it does work: we become driven to perform and achieve in order to avoid the self-judgement when we fail. However, sometimes it can be so terrifying that we don't even try. We avoid things we are not 'perfect' at or activities we are certain we can't fail in. This means many of us miss out on things in our lives that are good for us: learning new skills, trying new things and creating new or improving existing relationships.

Tina strove for perfection, yet perfection isn't attainable. Through our coaching sessions, we discussed how she really felt when she told herself she was 'useless', when something wasn't perfect. Tina began to see that being so critical towards herself was causing her harm, as well as affecting her relationships with those she cared about. It wasn't motivating and inspiring for her to listen to the words of her inner critic anymore.

Tina had achieved a great deal in the only way she knew to be with herself. However, these old patterns of behaviour weren't working for her any more. We discussed self-compassion and what it would mean to be kinder to herself – to stop judging and constantly evaluating herself. Initially, she felt really uncomfortable at the prospect. Tina shared a common feeling many of us have – that having self-compassion is an over-indulgent way to be – and feared that without her inner critic she wouldn't get things done. When I explained that it was about treating ourselves with the same kindness and compassion we would show a good friend or a child, she agreed to give it a go.

Gradually, she began to develop a more compassionate voice and identify that part of herself. She chose to keep a small photograph of her son on her desk at work where it was easily visible. This reminded her of what was most important in her life. Whenever she noticed her self-critical voice, she asked herself:

- What would I tell my son right now?

- What would be the most compassionate way for me to speak to *my* inner child right now?

An important part of our work together involved helping Tina find and turn up the volume on the compassionate part of herself. We identified what she really wanted, the type of person she wanted to be and alternative ways to her thinking about her situation whilst creating a path to move forward. Helping Tina to focus on her ideal self and a vision of who she would like to be was powerful for her. We explored two possible futures: one where she created compassion towards herself and another where she continued without any change. Positive visioning has been shown to be powerful in creating hope and guiding future behaviour. From this, we were able to identify and set goals to help Tina move towards her preferred vision.

Reflections

As my journey into compassion and coaching has developed, I have also noticed that I have become more compassionate towards myself. Witnessing and working alongside the transformation of somebody else is very powerful. Tina listening to her own internal critical voice also allowed me to identify blind spots and areas where I too was striving for perfection. Being able to acknowledge with my clients that being 'good enough' is okay, that we all have similar struggles and that I have also used support from others allows a deeper connection – one of shared experience, of shared humanity:

Rather, genuine compassion is based on the rationale that all human beings have an innate desire to be happy and overcome suffering, just like myself. And, just like myself, they have the natural right to fulfill this fundamental aspiration. On the basis of the recognition of this equality and commonality, you develop a sense of affinity and closeness with others. (Dalai Lama cited in Lama and Cutler 1998)

For me, there is no doubt that coaching and compassion go hand in hand, since both focus on building emotional resources rather than addressing old wounds, both help people discover and develop their inner strengths and resources and both help to improve resilience. Self-compassion provides the safety needed to be aware of, and acknowledge, our weaknesses and recognise that imperfection is part of being human. Self-compassion approaches and coaching both ask the question: 'What is good for *you*?'

As a psychologist, it has also been a freeing and more compassionate way for me to work. I have found that my inner critic is much quieter when I am coaching compared with when I am working as a therapist. I am aware that this could be for a number of reasons. Certainly, working with clients to assist them to become more compassionate towards themselves has a positive impact. Coaching has an impetus on promoting positive change and psychological wellbeing.

I often ask fewer questions about 'why' (Why did this happen? Why do you feel this way?) and more about 'how' (How can you think about this in a different way?) or 'what' (What would be best for you to do right now?). As a listener, hearing less of the client's story (the pain, trauma and emotion) means there is less opportunity for indirect exposure to pain and suffering. Learning from my own experience, I believe there is less opportunity for burnout when working in this way. When I coach, I feel I am using more compassion than empathy. Of course, both go hand in hand, but for me to help my clients, I don't need to hear, feel and understand what my client has experienced by attending to their story. Yet I do need to show compassion, to acknowledge their pain, to recognise our shared humanity, to say 'I hear you' and 'We're all in this together' and help them develop a less critical, more soothing, compassionate way of being.

Conclusion

Compassion is a core ingredient of positive change, either as a style or way of being in coaching. Boyatzis *et al.* (2010) have linked the implementation of a compassionate style of coaching to better coaching outcomes, showing that clients are more likely to learn and make significant behavioural changes in comparison with a more critical style of coaching. Helping clients to think about and grow into more of *who* they want to be, using compassion in coaching provides clients with an alternative way of thinking about their situation and their path moving forwards. Finally, research suggests that therapists who are trained in self-compassion are less likely to experience compassion fatigue because of the skills they have available to them to avoid getting burned out. Engaging with this way of working with clients has certainly helped me become a better psychologist, as well as a healthier and happier person.

References

Boyatzis, R., Jack, A., Cesaro, R., Passarelli, A. and Khawaja, M. (2010). *Coaching with Compassion: An fMRI Study of Coaching to the Positive or Negative Emotional Attractor.* Presented at the annual meeting of the Academy of Management, Montreal, Quebec, Canada.

Lama, D. and Cutler, H. C. (1998). *The Art of Happiness: A Handbook for Living.* New York: Riverhead Books.

Figley, C. R. (ed.) (1995). *Compassion Fatigue: Coping with Secondary Traumatic Stress Disorder in Those Who Treat the Traumatized.* Bristol, PA: Brunner/Mazel.

Maslow, A. H. (1968). *Toward a Psychology of Being.* New York: D. Van Nostrand Company.

Neff, K. D. (2003). Self-compassion: An alternative conceptualization of a healthy attitude toward onself. *Self and Identity, 2,* 85–102.

Palmer, S. and Whybrow, A. (2005). The proposal to establish a Special Group Coaching Psychology. *The Coaching Psychologist 1,* 5–12.

Rogers, C. R. (1961). *On Becoming a Person: A Therapist's View of Psychotherapy.* London: Robinson.

Ryan, R. M. and Deci, E. L. (2001). To be happy or to be self-fulfilled: A review of research on hedonic and eudaimonic well-being. In S. Fiske (ed.) *Annual Review of Psychology 52.* Palo Alto, CA: Annual Reviews/Inc.

Sabin-Farrell, R. and Turpin, G. (2003). Vicarious traumatization: Implications for the mental health of workers. *Clinical Psychology Review, 23,* 32–36.

Whitmore, S. J. (1992). *Coaching for Performance: A Practical Guide to Growing Your Own Skills.* London: Nicholas Bearley.

8

Between Being and Becoming

CHALLENGES AND RESOURCES
IN TRAINING THERAPISTS

Simone Bol

*Speech and Language Therapist, Senior Lecturer
and Trainee Counselling Psychologist*

Learning and teaching can be joyful activities and can help human beings to develop, grow and share and reflect on matters of importance to them. Still, I think most readers will share with me some fairly fearful memories related to education. Below I will reflect on my experiences around learning and teaching and self-compassion over the last couple of years. Currently, I am a trainee counselling psychologist, as well as a senior lecturer and external examiner in the area of clinical linguistics and speech and language therapy. My average working week encompasses a variety of different activities: I see clients, receive supervision, write case studies and essays, teach, examine and am examined both as a learner and teacher. I learn as a teacher from my students, as a clinician from my clients and supervisor and as a student from my tutors, and in all these contexts from my various peers.

I have encountered many challenges along the way and many moments in which self-compassion seemed to go out of the window a bit (or a lot). My developing psychological framework as a trainee counselling psychologist, which I will use in this chapter, includes aspects of humanistic approaches, psychodynamic understandings and Paul Gilbert's work on compassion. Taking an integrative stance, integrating my professional identities and models, I will discuss how these theoretical positions inform my reflections on my experiences.

Below I would like to try to unpack what makes compassion so challenging in educational contexts and how education and compassion can possibly exist together, peacefully, a little more often. For a basic understanding of compassion, I use Gilbert's framework that describes compassion as a basic kindness, an awareness of suffering of self and other and a wish to relieve this (Gilbert 2010). In his description of the affect regulation systems, Gilbert (2010) distinguishes three types of affect regulation systems that all have relevance for learning and teaching. The *activating system*, of pursuing and achieving, is clearly highly relevant for educational contexts. Then he describes the *threat-focused system*, which deals with fear and trying to keep out of harm's way. Obviously, learning and teaching in modern times is not deliberately attempting to activate this system, yet the experience of many learners, including myself, is that fear frequently plays a part in the experiences surrounding learning. Below I will draw on psychodynamic theory to explore this unintended and more difficult aspect of education. Finally, there is the *soothing and contentment system* that Gilbert associates with sharing, belonging, kindness and compassion, which is probably the most difficult system to relate directly to learning experiences, as it requires a state of *not-wanting*. Still, kindness and a focus on enjoying the company of others for its own sake can be found frequently in educational settings too.

I will start with the affect regulation systems that may be a thread to compassion, as understanding how these work may help to encapsulate the challenges education poses to us, which can help us to be more perceptive in moments of need for self-compassion. Being aware of these mechanisms can help to reduce self-blame.

Achieving and pursuing

The endeavour of education is most clearly linked with the achievement of learning objectives of one kind or another and the pursuit of particular aims. Students embark on a course to become something they are not yet. As a trainee applied psychologist, there is a constant sense that there is something that I am not yet but that I hope to become. Being a student puts one in a liminal, in-between state. When reading application forms as a tutor, it is clear many students are keen to follow a particular career path, and there has been a lead up to this point, a history and a particular future in mind. University education is a connection between a person's past and their future, and both play a part in recruitment and selection processes. The emphasis is on what have you done so far and where you want to be in the future.

Applicants, students and trainees are also expected to demonstrate a high level of motivation and dedication to the chosen path. This is of course fully justified considering the time, effort and finances required. In the case of trainee therapists, considering the importance of commitment for the public they will serve during placements and in their profession, demonstrating dedication is perhaps particularly important. Still, this emphasis on being sure about *wanting to become* may need a little closer inspection from a psychological point of view, as it might not do justice to the full experience of people's *selves*.

When being interviewed for my current course, I was asked the (rather mean!) question: 'What would you not like us to know about you?' My answer concerned my doubt, particularly about this certainty about my self-chosen study direction. I wanted to do a doctorate in counselling psychology, but on the other hand was I really sure about this? Looking back, writing this, I can see it was a rather humane answer, and I gather my assessors must have thought the same, because I was duly admitted to the programme. Yet, this is not what is put on the average successful application form, and probably a level of false certainty is felt to be needed and is then reinforced by competitive selection processes. Having to continue a façade of certainty is likely to involve an element of 'foreclosure' on the playfulness that is associated with curiosity in assuming a position and direction that is only starting to become real. Gilbert and Choden (2015) advocate curiosity and openness in dealing with challenges and anxieties. Furthermore, in line with Winnicott's (2005) thinking, development of the new identity is likely to be healthier, richer and more in tune if some playing around with it has been allowed. Putting a new identity, or the transitional student–professional identity, through a playful test of pulling it a bit apart, holding it upside down, tasting and squeezing it and maybe throwing it out of the pram – temporarily or not – might allow for more real and fitting professional identities to emerge. A robustness of educators facilitating curiosity, openness, challenge and change, as well as providing some perspective, is in my experience helpful in this process.

Being a mature student probably often leads initially to more self-doubt than that of many late-adolescent applicants to undergraduate degrees who may, on average, be a little more linearly convicted in their pursuits, with less experience of decisions not going to plan or working out. For mature students, pursuing a new career path is often a rather invested enterprise, as other commitments also need to be considered and held roles and identities need to be either given up or given less attention or significance than previously. This, in my experience, and reported by, for example, Shanahan (2000) and Baxter and Britton (2001), can add to the strain these students sometimes experience, as their pursuing is a rather loaded enterprise. Of course, I am one of these mature students and have not infrequently along the way wondered why on earth I am doing what I am doing. Still, I come to the conclusion that the pursuit is worthwhile. Being provided a space to be honest about these doubts, I would argue, helps us to be really engaged with the world we are in and to discuss out concerns with those around us.

Sometimes students come to a different conclusion about their chosen path, and, as tutor, I have been on the receiving end of these decisions. I often get a sense of profound shame around the decision to leave the course. Gilbert and Procter (2006) describe how self-criticism and non-favourable self-evaluation can lead to feelings of shame. Often, students report that they are not sure how to tell their parents, and in some cases their partner, about their decision. Introjected idealisations about desired outcomes and socially reinforced 'ways to be and to be purposeful' seem to hang over students as powerful internalised values and judges. In a situation where others are seen as more powerful, being self-critical and blaming the self can be a safety behaviour in order to avoid the powerful 'other' to do the punishment (Gilbert and Procter 2006).

There is the perceived expectation of knowing one's pursuits, yet sometimes a little 'trial and error' is a good thing. In 'learning organisations' (e.g. universities), changing paths and pursuits can be a very fruitful enterprise for individuals. Looking kindly at earlier decisions may be very helpful here. For example, I have introduced myself in the section above as someone engaged with various interesting achievements and pursuits, but have so far failed to tell you I am also a school dropout and have had many trials and tribulations. These include attempts at nursing and achieving secretarial skills (my lack of success at the latter will not surprise colleagues nor students). A version of a 'finished product' is often displayed, but it is not the full picture. 'Selfies', visual or in this case in written form, are scrutinised for a level of completion and perfection and don't often demonstrate to others the messiness of one's existence. Allowing for this, interpreting the messiness as humane, normal and constructive can then help a student to still feel a sense of belonging with all others who are 'plodding along as best as they can'. Hearing this from an educator who is often perceived as being in *loco parentis*, or as an otherwise idealised or at least judging authority figure, can sometimes help to shift the sense of shame and self-criticism to some extent. Of course, there are often time and cost implications and an acknowledgement that there is disappointment and sadness to leave and that sometimes things don't work out as hoped for is also often part of doing justice to this part of the experience for many people.

In psychotherapy work, I sometimes see a similar process. Clients often apologise at the beginning of the work about the messiness of their existence, telling me they have failed to achieve one or more life tasks. Looking for therapy is often felt as being a failure, and processes of shame are frequently explained at the beginning with a yet unknown, and therefore unsafe, other.

When pursued tasks are perceived as not having been achieved in education, there is often disappointment and self-blame, and a similar process as that outlined above then often takes place. Often this is accompanied by a fear of losing connections to people. Friends might have done better (choose your friends wisely!), so students often fear they don't properly belong in their circle of friends any more (and are 'not good enough'). There may be a threat of having to join another cohort if the year is not passed or possibly even having of to leave the course. Belonging to a group is part of people's sense of safety and a source of compassion – as I discuss shortly. Losing this is often felt very deeply. Most frequently, these fears temporarily spiral out of proportion at the time of disappointment and shame about a not-achieved aim. When students connect with others, be it friends, family or educators, about their disappointment and learn they are still accepted as a member of the fallible human race and the groups they belong to, fears about disconnection often alleviate. Sometimes, shame prevents students from seeking contact and disclosing, and this process can, in my experience, lead to students having a really difficult time and sometimes being significantly isolated. Making it clear to students that it is important to come and talk about disappointments right from the start of the course and reiterating this message can help to facilitate a safer and more constructive environment for learning and development. Disappointments are part of life but if they are hidden and a source of shame, they quickly get in the way of learning and development.

Fear in educational relations

A sense of anxiety or fear is often part of educational experiences. This has come to light a little already in the section above in relation to fear of not achieving or pursuing. I would like to unpack this a little more using a broadly psychodynamic framework. First of all, I will address the fears associated with *becoming*, then I will consider the interpersonal relations of learning and teaching and how fear may surface here.

The enterprise of education deals with learning a new skill, new knowledge and, in the case of vocational courses, a new identity. It also goes hand in hand with meeting new people and being in new roles. A learner is a 'beginner', and beginnings are associated with 'the unknown' – not quite knowing what you are exposing yourself to, or what is exposed about you, whilst finding out new rules and boundaries. In short, uncertainties are assured. There is something one does not yet know, is not yet able to do (well) and, for regulated professions, not yet allowed to do that is appealing and desired. There is a desire to achieve and become.

Desire and fear are often linked in psycho-analytic theory (Phillips 1997). To simplify quite radically, there is a desire to be able to do and know, yet also a fear of being expected (by self or others) to do and know. This is also a well-known theme in the existential tradition. *Becoming* can be a fearful business as well as being exciting. Fear and excitement are not far removed from each other. The actual emergence of anxiety in this tradition is seen as an unconscious defensive distraction from engaging with the content of fear and/or desire, as anxiety overpowers and distracts thereby from anything else. Both beginnings, as outlined above, and endings – when relationships, as they are known, come to an end and there is an expectation of having acquired and being able to face the world with a new identity (every ending is also a beginning) – can be demanding and bring this affect regulation system into play. Finishing a course, and even a piece of work along the way, can therefore be an anxiety-provoking activity, which not infrequently is subject to avoidance strategies. This can be seen, for example, in procrastination or rumination about a submission (e.g. 'Did I really include that appendix?' or 'Did I put enough of theory X in?').

Being in university education as an adult can, of course, bring back memories of childhood educational experiences, but it can also bring one back to an infantile state of being, dependent on the judgement and provision of 'bigger' people. Salzberger-Wittenberg (1983) describes how something of the anxious state and processes infants probably experience in their dependent position can also be seen in students and pupils at times. The infant-like state related to not knowing, being new, not knowing the environment and feeling powerless is generally particularly salient at the beginning of a new educational experience. I was particularly interested to learn about the splitting tendencies that students, including myself, often fall into. There is, as in all anxiety according to psycho-analytic literature, a need to hold on to the idealised 'parent' or authority figure, in this case a teaching professional, but also for someone to project fears and negative feelings onto them and see them as incapable in turn (the feeling the student needs to get rid of). Judgements can be strongly felt and extreme in content, from idealising to diminishing. These judgements can be applied to the self but also projected onto teaching professionals and peers.

Students often feel they are not 'sufficiently fed' information or knowledge. I experienced this on both sides, especially recently in my dual role of lecturer and learner: students who were very hungry for more guidance and me wanting more guidance from my course. This state of 'needing more' might be a type of 'suffering' that needs to be endured and be dealt with sympathetically but is not necessarily something that can be resolved. Feelings of one's own inadequacy can be projected onto others (Salzberger-Wittenberg 1983). In the current socio-political climate, students are often seen as 'customers'. Student evaluations, such as in the National Student Survey, but also many intermediate evaluations in relation to Continuous Improvement Plans and the like, have become a very strong driver in higher education. Listening to student experiences is a good thing, but experiences need to be placed in context, and tick boxes and Likert scales are not the most sophisticated instruments, particularly when designed without being able to take the design, timing and challenges of specific educational experiences into account. This can, at times, impede true dialogue, particularly when student concerns are mainly aired indirectly through various and increasingly numerous instruments, rather than face to face with the human being concerned. This can become anxiety-provoking for teaching professionals, as there is uncertainty about what is really going on and judgements and consequences can be rather impactful. This may contribute, if it becomes disproportionate, to a climate of fear rather than of mutual understanding.

For clients in therapy, the need to be 'fed' from a position of feeling powerless and anxious can manifest itself as 'wanting to know what to do', wanting a therapist to tell clients how to lead their life and wanting a therapist to be a role model. Being a trainee clinician in this respect is particularly interesting, as on the one hand, there is often a feeling of inadequacy as a learner, and on the other hand, there is a client who might idealise the therapist or at least want some clear answers and tips. The latter of course needs careful consideration, as a therapist may want to provide help and assistance depending on their therapeutic stance but may not want to be too directive and tell a client how to lead their life, taking over a client's sense of agency. To some extent, this will be dependent on the modality that is foregrounded in the therapeutic work: a Cognitive Behaviour Therapy approach allows for more directive work, a relational psychodynamic approach for much less.

In the cognitive behavioural literature, some 'splitting' phenomena may be explained from a different or complementary theoretical understanding as black-and-white thinking and narrowing of thoughts as a natural response to anxiety-provoking situations. These sort of processes are certainly also relevant when it concerns academic work of students dealing with anxiety. The psychodynamic literature explains the strong emotional responses that can occur towards the people involved, the educators or 'authority' figures. Reading about this has helped me reflect on my own experiences and be a little kinder to my own 'childish' responses. As both a student and a lecturer, I found myself wondering about my responses and being a little irritated by myself at times. Understanding these mechanisms can help to reduce self-blame and increase compassion with those hungry to be fed information and knowledge.

Compassion and self-soothing

After outlining the affect regulation systems, which at times challenge and compete with self-compassion, I would now like to reflect on where and how I have experienced sharing, the *not-wanting* and compassion. The most obvious place to start is peer and general people support. Face-to-face education, and probably other means of communication too, allow for a meeting of minds and hearts. In professional education, it is not uncommon for students to report for the first time meeting others with similar interests and dispositions. Students often comment on how friendly peers are and, in my own recent experience as a trainee, this is still pivotal in getting through one's course. Belonging to a group and a community of learners can foster compassion. It highlights similarities, allows difference and facilitates compassion with others and self. A sense of safety can be derived from being around others who can care and watch out for us. Spontaneous social activities often emerge on Thursday evenings, Halloween and various other points in the academic year. Salzberger-Wittenberg (1983) describes how sibling rivalry can be a part of peer groups, and Gilbert (2010) describes potential challenges of togetherness, such as (self-) pressure to conform. Allowing for differences between individuals, and doing so deliberately and consciously in educational settings, as well as allowing for different forms of togetherness, seems a good way to reap the benefits of togetherness and belonging without stifling individuality and genuineness. In my own training as a therapist, there is a lot of attention to group processes, and learning about similarities and differences in emotional experiences are enhancing and supportive and provide a rich experience of humanity.

Relations with other 'alleged' humans, such as teaching staff, can also create a compassionate environment. In lectures, students, including myself, often perk up when a little personal anecdote is shared or a glimpse is provided about an educator's personal life. Humans want to connect to humans. I recently shared my own failure at an assessment with an anxious student who came to me for a tutorial after a failed assessment, and the effect was remarkable. I would not recommend this in every situation, but like in therapeutic encounters, well-judged self-disclosure can be very useful on occasion. A little humbleness from academics can probably go a long way and make people more at ease with having to overcome difficulties as part of learning. And isn't overcoming difficulties and challenges not just the essence of learning?

Harvey and Delfabbro (2004) consider the factors contributing to the development of resilience in developing young people. They consider both Bronfenbrenner's ecological model, which focuses on social environmental influences such as educational establishments, and Bandura's social-cognitive and self-efficacy theories. Students can at times 'borrow' from the experiences and make meaning from others, particularly if they are deemed to be similar to themselves and are in a perceived position of what they describe as 'dominance'. In psycho-analytic terminology, this process may be described as 'introjection of values' in a relationship in which there is a level of attachment.

In an academic professional therapy training compassion is also part of the content of the curriculum. The new knowledge and skills are acquired with the view of helping others, and learning to understand perspectives from people having different life experiences is an important part of this. In speech and language therapy, the aim is to help others to connect to people around them by assisting communication. In applied psychology training, we aim to understand others and nurture concern for their wellbeing. Personal histories and motivations come into choosing these professional pathways, and considerations of these are important in training. Learning about humanity can also contribute to self-compassion in various ways.

I also wonder, though, whether connecting with human beings at another level is also often achieved by the curriculum. For instance, the knowledge and literature transmitted and investigated connects us to fellow human beings who have thought, written and debated. Through engagement with the curriculum, students can discover a connection with more abstract and not personally known human minds. Any area of academic learning connects and reflects on other people's thinking and motives. Being able to engage with the content at hand from a sharing and discovering point of view, rather than an achievement-driven position, will aid enjoyment of learning and reduce strain on mental health. Educational thinkers such as Rogoff (see for example Rogoff and Toma 1997) emphasise the collaborative nature of learning, and the social–historical perspective on learning and development emphasises that it involves a process of learning to share the tools of human traditions and to be part of those (Vygotsky 1978). Many educationalists from Montessori to Bruner (1986) also emphasise the joy of discovery and curiosity in learning.

Learning from practice placements is another area for the development of compassion. As a trainee applied psychologist, empathising with some level of stress and insecurities is a relatively easy part of the job when working with clients. This material is quite to hand in one's life as a trainee, who is assessed and rightly judged for performing sufficiently well in client care. I have found sources of support in the people I connect with, the peers, tutors and clients. It is a humbling and enriching experience to connect with clients and to understand more about the course content and human existence in general through real-life experience and individuals' stories and experiences. My own clinical placements help me to understand the course content for real, and in my students I often see a lot of personal development and deepening of understanding when they go on placements and can connect with real people in their work. This process probably merits a chapter in its own right.

I take a relational approach in client work where, in the service of the client's needs, a therapist can be a real human being and fosters mental health as also outlined by Gilbert (2010). This is also challenging for a trainee therapist. In psychological therapy training, the self is – rightly and necessarily – under scrutiny and shaken up, sometimes by mandatory or elective personal therapy but also by the content of the curriculum. Reading and investigating crucial and impactful aspects of human life, such as attachment relations and styles, anxiety and bereavement are part of not just the client's life but that of every human being. Memories are triggered and held assumptions about the self are seen in a different light and this can be disturbing, enriching and/or questioning. Assignments on my course often require personal reflections, and getting these back with critiques and comments from authority figures can feel like an attack to the self at times. Gilbert (2010) discusses in this respect how self-reflection or 'the curse of the self' can trigger basic emotional state of 'alertness to danger' and 'pursuit' and in particular might make us compare ourselves to others. Sussing out similarities and differences is basic cognitive pattern seeking and also part of meeting new people in any setting or group. It is an important cognitive and social cognitive skill, but where it concerns the self and others it often has emotional consequences. The anxiety of being different, 'not good enough' and not belonging can, in my experience, be heightened by continuous self-reflection. When someone is developing this skill, the self-image is changed and can be challenged. Self-reflection can become a pattern of self-doubt or excessive worry if it is not embedded in kindness and allowance for difference, incompleteness and messiness. Humour can play a role in this, as it allows for playful manipulation of loose ends, multiple levels of interpretation and creative distance, as well as emotional release. Sometimes there has been enough analysis and reflection for the day, and it is time to go to the pub (or curl up on the sofa or simply lie down in a darkened room!). Self-reflection can also aid resilience, for example, Harvey and Delfabbro (2004) point out it can allow for a sense of having a level of understanding of self and relationships and responses to others and, as Gilbert (2010) maintains, it can therefore be an important tool to reduce harm to self and others when applied well and in good measure.

Staying attuned to others' needs whilst all this is going on when in training can be quite a task, so self-care and self-compassion are necessities for carrying out clinical work well. I will return to this topic at the end of this chapter.

Organisational challenges

Taking into account the challenges and opportunities for developing and sustaining compassion in the continuing education of health professionals, I would like to reflect briefly on organisational structures. There is currently a lot of emphasis on the student experience in higher education, and organisational structures arise to consider and enhance this. It is laudable and compassionate to consider people's experience but where and how this happens is important considering the emotions involved in teaching and learning. As splitting between good and bad, trustworthy and potentially threatening, providing and demanding, is an understandable, though primitive and often misguided, response to the anxieties education can provoke, I would argue that educators still need to be very much involved in dealing with student experience as and when it happens as part of the learning process. Too much organisational splitting between learning and 'being' or experiencing will only reinforce anxieties in the learning process, as it provides a structure to avoid the cause of fear.

Specialised roles have a place in large organisations, and professional, confidential counselling has an important role in higher education for those with individual concerns and needs, but the experience of the learning process as such is part of the education process and part of the relationship between students and educators. Organisational structures, professional roles and physical (who thought open-plan offices were a good idea?!) and/or virtual environments can facilitate this or inhibit this, for example by making an environment more or less personal and conducive to contact. This is not an easy thing to get right, but it is worth aiming for. Large organisations have their challenges and may at times impose measure or measurements that challenge connecting with people at a humane level, as I have discussed above in relation to teaching evaluation. Large higher education institutions can also offer many opportunities to learn about the diversity of human experience through the variety of disciplines they bring together and can bring people together in unexpected and novel ways. Celebrating these opportunities as and when they occur can add excitement and contribute to the opportunity to develop resilience in dealing with the more challenging aspects, within a fairly safe environment.

The splitting of roles in the health service, between, for example, therapists and assistants, assessors and providers of therapies, also needs to be considered for its merit and challenges to the work that is being undertaking and the relationships provided for clients. Compassionate relationships arise from dealing with the positive and negative. It requires genuineness not to impose or cajole towards agendas and to allow for harder experiences to be seen and tolerated. Harvey and Delfabbro (2004) suggest resilience can enhance an ability for tolerance through enhancing protective factors such as providing a supportive community, allowing for difference and diversity and reducing risk factors. Risk, in this sense, refers to employees not feeling acknowledged and valued and being depleted, stressed and quite possibly anxious, hampering them in providing good care.

To provide good-quality care, professionals need to be trained well and courses and students/trainees need to meet criteria of competency and quality. There is ultimately a necessary element of judgement in education. To foster a compassionate mindset, engagement with the curriculum content could benefit from a position of curiosity and discovery, rather than from attempting to meeting external criteria. This means there are some conflicting aspects to teaching and particularly to assessment. Allowing playfulness, genuine interest and discovery into assessment fosters a self-compassionate mindset, which will enhance resilience. As an educator, I try to live by the adage 'There are many ways of being right' and in terms of judgement/marking, 'If it is not wrong, it is right.' As a student and trainee, I often still prefer structured guidelines and clear tick boxes, yet ultimately I believe more growth and learning happen from intrinsically motivated enjoyment of exploration of the material at hand. Dealing with the uncertainty of opportunities is worth our effort in my opinion.

Resilience through compassion

Being a practitioner psychologist trainee or a therapy student on placement provides a person with many opportunities to develop compassion. Learning about people's life experiences and their perspectives, learning to reflect on one's own experiences and considering these, learning about thinking about people's development, difficulties and communication and meeting similarly minded people are just some of these opportunities. Yet the process of becoming, being new and inexperienced and that of being assessed compete and sometimes conflict with a compassionate state of mind and this is particularly required in therapy training.

Insight into the complexities of this process can help trainees and other students to be more self-compassionate. Looking after oneself is particularly important to prevent burnout. Self-care is crucial. It can be helpful to allow for the uncertainty involved with every change, put the necessary achievements into perspective, enjoy the discovery of learning and, last but not least, facilitate the connection to other people in ways that work well.

Educators and educational institutions need to juggle the competing demands of organising the learning, teaching and assessment environment in manners that foster (self-) compassion and still do the job of an educational establishment within a particular political environment. Resilience can be enhanced by providing opportunities to reflect and connect in ways that allow a level uncertainty and diversity and stimulate exploration.

References

Baxter, A. and Britton, C. (2001). Risk, identity and change: Becoming a mature student. *International Studies in Sociology of Education, 11*(1), 87–104.

Bruner, J. (1986). *Actual Minds, Possible Worlds*. Cambridge, MA: Harvard University Press.

Gilbert, P. (2010). *The Compassionate Mind*. London: Constable.

Gilbert, P. and Choden, P. (2015). *Mindful Compassion*. London: Robinson.

Gilbert, P. and Procter, S. (2006). Self criticism: Overview and pilot study of a group therapy approach. *Clinical Psychology and Psychotherapy, 13*, 353–379.

Harvey, J. and Delfabbro, P. H. (2004). Psychological resilience in disadvantaged youths: A critical overview. *Australian Psychologist, 39*(1), 3–13.

Phillips, A. (1997). *Terrors and Experts*. Cambridge, MA: Harvard University Press.

Rogoff, B. and Toma, C. (1997). Shared thinking: Community and institutional variations. *Discourse Processes, 23*(3), 471–497.

Salzberger-Wittenberg, I. (1983). 'Hopeful and Fearful Beginnings.' In I. Salzberger-Wittenberg, G. Williams and E. Osborne (eds) *The Emotional Experience of Learning and Teaching.* New York: Routledge and Kegan Paul Ltd.

Shanahan, M. (2000). Being that bit older: Mature students' experience of university and healthcare education. *Occupational Therapy International, 7*(3), 153–162.

Vygotsky, L. (1978). *Mind in Society. New Edition.* Cambridge, MA: Harvard University Press.

Winnicott, D. W. (2005). *Playing and Reality.* London: Routledge.

9

Compassion in Clinical Psychology Training

Dr Jenny Shuttleworth Davies

Clinical Psychologist and Clinical Tutor

Love and compassion are necessities, not luxuries. Without them humanity cannot survive.

Dalai Lama

I feel as if I've always known this. Or maybe I should say I know that I've always felt this. Because that's where this understanding lies: nestled in that place where feelings and thoughts are one. That place of early experience where we emerge into the world and begin our own journey of sense-making. Where we require the care of an 'other' to survive, where abandonment would mean death and where, if we are fortunate enough, we are bathed in another's love and care that holds us through the most terrifying moments.

Hello. I'm Jen. I'm a clinical psychologist and a tutor on the Lancaster University clinical psychology training programme. I'm some other things as well, but it is from my experiences in this particular role that this chapter is written. I am going to be writing about the development of compassionate mind training (CMT) groups in our course community. I will start with a consideration of the context in which the clinical psychology training course sits, provide a brief account of my journey into the world of CMT and then expand on the joys and challenges of facilitating compassion-focused groups with trainee clinical psychologists.

Two worlds

Clinical psychology training is a funny old place, a community that exists in both the worlds of academia and healthcare. We are not alone in inhabiting this position of course. There are other training courses that have one foot in the National Health Service (NHS) and the other in a university setting, where trainees are negotiating and balancing the role of being a student with the responsibility of being a healthcare professional.

Existing across these domains brings great opportunities: opportunities to learn and develop and to build meaningful theory–practice links. It also brings challenges, as these two worlds have a tendency for 'drive'. Essentially, they are about 'doing', 'striving' and 'achieving'. And rightly so; the NHS keeps people alive and healthy by doing, striving and achieving. Great leaps in knowledge within the world of academia come about because of doing, striving and achieving. Drive is not problematic per se. Problems arise when drive is over-stimulated by the context in which we find ourselves (Pani 2000) and when, through a complex interaction with the threat system, it costs us in terms of our capacity to soothe and be soothed (Figure 9.1).

Figure 9.1 Emotional regulation systems: the compassionate mind approach

Fundamentally, the argument here is that within both the NHS and the education system in the UK, we have created a context that exercises and strengthens the threat and the drive system to such an extent that the soothing system suffers.

In education, we start young with assessment regimes in primary schools that many teachers believe prevent meaningful learning. Twenty-five years on from when the first SATS (National Curriculum assessments) were introduced, 90 per cent of teachers state that preparation for these tests negatively impacts children's wellbeing, mental health and self-confidence (National Union of Teachers [NUT] 2016). The threat system is at large within the educational system. It affects the pupils and it affects the teachers, with reports of 'soaring' stress levels amongst school staff (British Broadcasting Corporation [BBC] 2015a).

And it is not just in the early years. For those who remain within education and move into academia, the threat continues to lurk. A recent study involving 14,000 university employees reported that, amongst academics, stress levels are growing and emotional wellbeing is deteriorating (Kinman and Wray 2013). This is in the context of heavy workloads, a 'long hours' culture and conflicting management demands. The 'threat' system is fed and grows as 'shoulds', 'oughts' and 'musts' function to fuel a desire to avoid feared negative events (Gilbert 2009).

The same goes for the NHS. In a world where healthcare trusts operate as businesses, target-driven bureaucracy and cost limitation take precedence (Cole-King and Gilbert 2011) and the threat system thrives. A week rarely goes by without mention by some news outlet of cuts to the NHS impacting negatively on patient care and staff wellbeing. In the past four years, staff absences for mental health problems have doubled at hospital trusts across England as reports of anxiety, stress and depression grow (BBC 2015b).

Failures are highlighted, people responsible for failures are sought and consequences (punishments) are promised. In the wake of the public enquiry into the Mid-Staffordshire Hospital Trust and the response to the Francis report from the government (Powell 2013), the language of shame has been used in an attempt to motivate change. And, of course, people died and that was unacceptable. Yet the question remains: Will increasing the threat level amongst staff and admonishing them for not being caring ever achieve the desired outcome of creating a safer and more compassionate workforce?

Bringing a compassionate approach to the situation

Various authors have argued for a different sort of intervention. In Sue Gerhardt's book *The Selfish Society: How We All Forgot to Love One Another and Made Money Instead* she argues that 'we live in an impoverished emotional culture, the end product of decades of individuation and consumerism, which have eroded our social bonds' (Gerhardt 2010, p.12). Her central tenant is that capitalism and an emphasis on rationalisation have influenced the way we parent and that this in turn has reduced our capacity as a society to truly understand others and ourselves as emotional beings and to connect to each other in helpful ways.

In a similar vein, in their book *Intelligent Kindness*, Ballatt and Campling debunk the idea that the 'promotion of competition and individualism in politics and economics, as well as in social and personal life…[is a] benign, creative and even natural…road to well-being' (2011, p.13). They highlight the misapplication of Darwinian Theory, which they argue actually emphasises human kinship as an evolutionary reality. They remind their readers that the NHS was established after World War II where British people had fought and died for the sake of the common good. They argue that the NHS was based on kinship and kindness and that, financially, as well as morally and ethically, a return to these concepts is needed.

In both *The Selfish Society* and *Intelligent Kindness*, the authors are arguing for organisational and societal change but on a supremely human level. Organisations and society are made up of people, people who interact with each other, people who require love and kindness to function at their best, people who feel guilt and can self-correct if they experience compassion, people who will withdraw into the threat system if they experience shame-based attacks.

The Harvard Business Report provides an example of this thinking in action. In 2015, the chief executive officer of Lakeland healthcare system in Michigan was driven to improve patient satisfaction ratings. However, he made a crucial decision that changes needed to come from the heart rather than the head:

> We're going to raise our scores by touching the hearts of our patients – by making sure they know not only how well we care for them, but how much we care about them. We're going to learn to be more loving. To do that, he said, I want to challenge you to bring your heart to work in new and creative ways. (Hamel 2015)

He reminded people of the reasons they had come in to that line of work and he reminded them of what it could feel like to be on the receiving end of healthcare: the process of admission, the treatment, the discharge. He did not assume he had to teach his staff how to do things differently, instead he trusted them to build 'heart-felt connections' with patients at these different stages and he encouraged them to share their stories with him and each other.

It worked. Not only did the patient satisfaction ratings soar but the clinical benefits were also evident:

> We are in the business of saving lives, of enhancing health, of restoring hope. When we touch the hearts of our patients we create a healing relationship that generates a relaxation response, lowers the blood pressure, improves the happy neurotransmitters, reduces pain, and improves outcomes – for both the patient and the caregiver. (Hamel 2015)

I read about this innovation when a good friend and colleague of mine tweeted about it. I felt a lump in my throat and tears prick my eyes as I read about the nurse who had intervened when security had been called to remove a distressed husband. She had asked if she could hug him. It made me pause and ask myself: How many heart-felt connections do I make on a daily basis? How often do I facilitate people to move out of their threat system to somewhere more soothing?

There has been evidence that schools adopting mindfulness, an approach that allows people to move into the soothing system rather than the threat or drive systems, have seen a positive impact not only on wellbeing but also on subsequent performance.[1] Although mindfulness is not about 'achieving', these outcomes have been welcomed by the education system. There appears to be a growing acknowledgement within the world of academia that there are benefits to moving away from a competitive model and becoming more connected with self and others. Or, perhaps these views are long held and it is just that social media is allowing them to be shared more widely. In 2014, the ethnographer Anne Galloway tweeted: 'Best advice I got when I entered academia: "We're all smart. Distinguish yourself by being kind."' Thousands of likes and retweets later, we may assume this struck a chord with many... including me.

---

1   See https://mindfulnessinschools.org for details of the research evidence.

My journey into compassionate mind work

My first introduction to compassionate mind training was when I heard Michelle Cree talking at a perinatal event (Cree 2015). I was blown away. I had been working in an early years' service for a few years with families from the point of pregnancy. The theoretical concepts both fitted with and expanded my understanding of the world and that was immediately attractive. I could see how useful this framework could be for my work as well as for me personally.

However, the most compelling element for me was Michelle herself. She personified compassion. She was, to borrow from the Circle of Security approach, 'bigger, stronger, wiser and kind' (Powell *et al.* 2013). She talked about the struggle of human existence genuinely, placing herself within it. She had a steadiness and warmth but most importantly a real strength that, in part, appeared to exist because of her capacity to embrace her own and other people's vulnerability.

It may seem strange to focus so much on one person but I think actually this is a key strength of the compassionate mind approach when it is used well. It makes it personal. It locates us all within the human experience. When used well, it allows people to connect.

I left that event determined to find a way to learn more and I was lucky enough to secure supervision from Michelle as I embarked on some perinatal work using this approach. I was struck by the power of CMT when working with families that had experienced huge levels of threat, such as domestic violence and child protection processes. It became part of how I operated as a clinician and as I left this post and took up the role of clinical tutor at the university, I wanted to keep it alive. I recognised the benefits that engaging in compassionate practice brought me on a personal level and I also felt that the course setting (as detailed above) was a place of high threat and that the approach may be of use to trainees negotiating their way through training.

Compassionate mind personal development groups

One of the roles I was given when I joined the staff team at Lancaster was to lead on the Personal Development and Reflection (PDR) teaching strand for our trainee clinical psychologists. A small team of us developed a strategy where trainees had access to various experiential opportunities for PDR throughout training. Our aim was that by the time they reached their third and final year, the trainees could choose to fill their protected

PDR teaching time with activities that worked for them. We are now in our fifth year of facilitating CMT groups as part of this final year.

The structure and content

We have six PDR teaching sessions over the trainees' third year, which means that we meet every couple of months. There are generally six to eight trainees in each group, and a staff member facilitates the group. On the first day we spend time establishing group contracts and thinking about safety within the experience. We then explore the theory behind a compassionate mind approach and start with some experiential exercises exploring the power of the mind and how body posture can influence experience and subsequent behaviour. We then move on to some exercises around compassionate attention/mindfulness, and we finish by planning how we will keep compassion alive between sessions – each of us committing to try something.

In the second session, we move on to compassionate imagery, the third session is focused on understanding and formulating ourselves using a compassionate frame and the fourth session devotes time to understanding how the self-critic and shame have come to play a role in our lives. Our fifth session involves compassionate letter writing to ourselves and then our final session in this PDR strand is a presentation day where the trainees talk about an aspect of their personal journey through training and we say our goodbyes.

Facilitation and supervision

The structure and the content of the groups came mainly from conversations in supervision with Michelle. Securing this supervision was a hugely important part of the process. Cole-King and Gilbert (2011) write about how compassion operates in the NHS (see Figure 9.2).

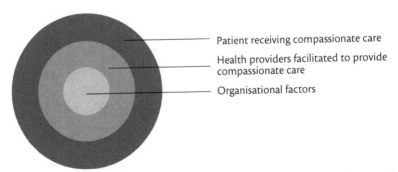

Figure 9.2 Influences upon Compassionate Healthcare (Cole-King and Gilbert 2011)

In order for the patient at the centre of the health provision to receive care that is compassionate, the providers of that care (the front-line staff) need to be able to offer a genuinely compassionate mindset and that is dependent on their training and the work environments that support them. This is, in turn, dependent on the organisation's qualities, values and demands.

As course staff members and facilitators, my colleagues and I were hoping to provide experiences in the CMT groups to support trainees in the development of their compassion for themselves and others. Receiving compassionate supervision from Michelle, as well as having the support of our clinical director, Anna Daiches, was crucial. We needed to experience compassion in order to offer it.

One of the things that struck me about the supervision that I received around the compassionate mind groups was the focus on me and my experiences within it. Process was hugely important. How to do things was discussed but much more important was that the supervision itself was compassionate. The model was lived. I'd raise a struggle I was facing in facilitating the groups and that struggle would be acknowledged and really examined, compassion would be brought to bear on it and the 'solutions' or the means to sit with the struggle would arise from that.

At the beginning, I'd find myself apologising for filling the space with my experiences and Michelle would respond with the words 'That's the work.' It took a while for me to genuinely believe this. But that is one of the 'truths' about compassion-focused work – or at least it is one of my truths. Compassion is not something you can 'do' to someone else. As Brené Brown points out in her TED talk on 'The Power of Vulnerability': 'We can't practice compassion with other people if we can't treat ourselves kindly' (Brown 2010).

We are wired for compassion and affiliative relationships from birth (Gilbert 2010) and yet we can get trained out of it (Oakes 2013). Many of us who enter the clinical psychology profession have developed our compulsive caregiving of others to a tee (Leiper and Casares 2000), and this can appear to cost us in terms of our capacity to care for ourselves. However, what we know is that we need to be able to apply the compassion and care to ourselves to prevent burnout and when we are able to do this the outcome is better for all involved (Braunschneider 2013).

The challenges and the rewards

So, how do we generally fare as a group of people in clinical psychology embarking on this compassionate journey together? Where do our challenges lie and what are the successes that we experience? I think one of the main issues we face is that we are doing this as part of a training course. This brings with it various challenges.

A large part of the clinical psychology training course involves the development of clinical skills. There can be a pull towards this in the compassionate mind PDR groups, a 'distancing' from self and a move towards the comfort of being the professional who applies this technique with others, rather than the human who struggles in similar ways and could do with embracing the techniques themselves. For example, in the session on compassionate formulation, the exercise where we apply this thinking to an 'other' (a case example) often comes with much greater ease than the section where we spend time formulating ourselves. We, as facilitators, perhaps collude with this tendency to think of the groups as an opportunity to develop clinically (rather than personally) useful skills. We call the groups 'compassionate mind training' groups rather than 'compassion-focused therapy' groups. We chose this title to emphasise the benefit of practising between sessions and also to underline that what we were offering is not therapy per se.

And this links with another of the challenges. We, as facilitators, are course staff members. In this context, we are trainers not therapists. We are associated with other elements of training, including the assessment process and, at times, this assessment process can represent a real threat. This means we, as facilitators, can represent a real threat too.

Other elements of the groups can also trigger threat responses, for example the aforementioned practice between sessions. Each time we meet, group members talk about how they are going to keep compassion alive between sessions, and we check in to see how this has gone in the following session. This has the potential to be shame inducing if people struggle to do what they had hoped to do and there is a danger that it becomes another stick for the self-critic to use. Similarly, the PDR presentation we do at the end of the year, which, although it is not assessed, is mandatory, can feel exposing and judging and it can function to exercise the 'drive' and 'threat' systems in unhelpful ways.

So, how do we address these challenges? It may sound simple or soft to say 'by embracing compassion'. But it is not. As Paul Gilbert and Michelle Cree emphasise in all their training, compassion is not an easy option. And this is where we return to the importance of compassionate supervision, offering this to each other as peer facilitators and accessing external support when possible. As a facilitator, I embarked on this journey as one that met my needs as well as the trainees', and I had a real desire to be the most compassionate version of me I could be. This means practising compassion, turning towards rather than away from the difficult stuff and being vulnerable at times.

And so we don't turn away. In the groups, we always try to name potential difficulties. We talk about the challenges of having a staff member as a facilitator, we discuss how the threat system can be activated by being in such a group in a training context and by practising (or not) between sessions. The clear contracting at the beginning, around what we want the group to be like and what role each of us wants to play, has been a crucial part of this process and revisiting this each session has helped us hold a safe frame. We bring compassion to bear on the situation we find ourselves in. We say to each other 'Of course that's how we feel, that's what our brains do.'

We discuss how we are going to support each other between sessions, and the groups I've facilitated have opted for a regular 'compassionate email reminder' from me as facilitator. We explicitly talk about the role of shame and the good intentions of the self-critic when it arises and admonishes us for not doing what we set out to do. We emphasise the okay-ness of us all as human beings regardless of how we are faring by other measures of success on the course. We encourage each other to participate at a level that works for us.

And the outcome? Well, this varies for different people but generally we see a growth in compassion. This shows itself in various ways. We complete measures of compassion at the beginning and the end of the year and, most often, these show a shift in a positive direction. One of my favourite moments in a group was when the members chose to share with each other that their scores hadn't changed. Together, they discussed how of course this would be the case given the stage of training they were at and they reflected on how the measures might capture something about what they were experiencing at that time but not necessarily say something fundamental about them as human beings. It was 'compassion in action' and it was wonderful watching their realisation grow that completing the questionnaires at the beginning of the year may have triggered more of a threat response, whereas at the end they were drawing on their compassionate resources to understand their situation.

Other favourite moments have been when group members have chosen to do something for their PDR presentation that has allowed them to be vulnerable and to 'really be seen' by the group, which Brené Brown describes as necessary for true connection with others (Brown 2010). We have had trainees playing musical instruments and knowing they will make mistakes, telling their story through the medium of 'geeky film quotes' or drawings they have done but would never normally show anyone, and trainees turning up to present without having prepared anything and saying 'I'm just going to be me.' These things took real courage and a capacity to be compassionate with self and trust in the compassion of the group. Compassion does seem to grow and spread, and I think the trainees become more active in this process over time. For example, they often start sharing compassionate moments, film clips, websites or articles with each other between sessions and/or encouraging each other to call on their compassionate others ('What would Brené do?').

My personal learning

I feel exceptionally grateful that I have had the opportunity to facilitate compassionate mind groups as part of my work. The practice of compassion is one that enhances my personal and professional life greatly. In terms of my development, I have found over time that I have shared more of me as a facilitator: more of my struggles and more of the moments of compassion that I've experienced in life. This has not been without risk, and I'm not sure I always get the balance right, but the beauty of the compassionate approach is it allows this to be named and explored. I am aware of the power I hold in the role as facilitator and that my task is to provide as safe a space as possible. My learning has been that acknowledging vulnerability within this, as an essentially human experience, has increased my capacity to do just that.

Another important bit of learning that has been confirmed by my experiences of facilitating these groups has been the influence of context. As outlined in the introduction, the NHS and university systems are not always the most compassionate of places to be. In addition to offering compassionate mind groups for trainees, I feel we still have work to do on changing some of our processes so that the environment we provide offers space for real learning and compassionate self-correction. Fortunately, I'm in a workplace where I feel we are making headway with these changes. And even in the moments when this feels too big a task, I remember another of my favourite quotes from the Dalai Lama and so I will finish with this: 'If you think you are too small to make a difference, try sleeping with a mosquito.'

References

Ballatt, J. and Campling, P. (2011). *Intelligent Kindness: Reforming the Culture of Healthcare.* London: RCPsych.

Braunschneider, H. (2013). Preventing and managing compassion fatigue and burnout in nursing. *ESSAI, 11,* (11). Available at http://dc.cod.edu/essai/vol11/iss1/11, accessed on 20 February 2017.

BBC (2015a). *Teacher Stress Levels in England 'Soaring', Data Shows.* Available at www.bbc.co.uk/news/education-31921457, accessed on 20 February 2017.

BBC (2015b). *Hospital Staff Absences for Mental Health Reasons Double.* Available at www.bbc.co.uk/news/uk-england-32022114, accessed on 20 February 2017.

Brown, B. (2010). *The Power of Vulnerability* [TED talk]. Available at www.ted.com/talks/brene_brown_on_vulnerability, accessed on 20 February 2017.

Cole-King, A. and Gilbert, P. (2011). Compassionate care: The theory and the reality. *Journal of Holistic Healthcare, 8*(3), 29–37.

Cree, M. (2015). *The Compassionate Mind Approach to Postnatal Depression: Using Compassion Focused Therapy to Enhance Mood, Confidence and Bonding.* London: Robinson.

Gerhardt, S. (2010). *The Selfish Society: How We All Forgot to Love One Another and Made Money Instead.* London: Simon and Schuster.

Gilbert, P. (2009). Introducing compassion focussed therapy. *Advances in Psychiatric Treatment, 15,* 199–208.

Gilbert, P. (2010). *The Compassionate Mind.* London: Constable.

Hamel, G. (2015). *Innovation Starts with the Heart, not the Head.* Available at https://hbr.org/2015/06/you-innovate-with-your-heart-not-your-head, accessed on 20 February 2017.

Pani, L. (2000). Is there an evolutionary mismatch between the normal physiology of the human dopaminergic system and current environmental conditions in industrialized countries? *Molecular Psychiatry, 5,* 467–475.

Kinman, G. and Wray, S. (2013). *Higher Stress: A Survey of Stress and Wellbeing among Staff in Higher Education.* London: UCU Publications.

Leiper, R. and Casares, P. (2000). An investigation of the attachment organization of clinical psychologists and its relationship to clinical practice. *British Journal of Medical Psychology, 73,* 449–464.

NUT (2016). *The Crisis in Primary Assessment: NUT Survey.* Available at www.teachers.org.uk/news-events/press-releases-england/crisis-primary-assessment-nut-survey, accessed on 20 February 2017.

Oakes, P. (2013). *Crash! Who Cares: Does our Training Contribute to the Culture of Cruelty in Health and Social Care Services?* Group of trainers in clinical psychology conference, Lancaster.

Powell, T. (2013). *The Francis Report (Report of the Mid-Staffordshire NHS Foundation Trust Public Inquiry) and the Government's Response.* Available at http://researchbriefings.files.parliament.uk/documents/SN06690/SN06690.pdf, accessed on 20 February 2017.

Powell, B., Cooper, G., Hoffman, K. and Marvin, B. (2013). *The Circle of Security Intervention: Enhancing Attachment in Early Parent–Child Relationships.* New York: Guilford Press.

PART FOUR

Making Space for Hope, Nurturing Resilience and Holding on to Compassion

Sarah Parry

The main aim of this book was to slow down and explore the experience of practising compassion for health and social care practitioners, to see how it might restore practitioner wellbeing, enhance service delivery and facilitate understanding around how compassion can operationalise hope and resilience as mechanisms of wellbeing. Storytelling and curiosity in a safe and reflexive space can be of great benefit to us as practitioners; it can enhance our capacity for empathy, increase our overall wellbeing, reduce the likelihood of burnout and enhance service delivery and service user satisfaction (Kapoulitsas and Corcoran 2015; Krasner *et al.* 2009; Raab 2014). With this in mind, the authors have generously shared their experiences of implementing and practising compassion, reflecting on the power of shared compassion between people, resulting in a rich tapestry of personal narratives from practice, illustrating the complexities and utility of compassionate practice. It is my hope that this collection of stories and reflections will contribute to our shared understanding of nurturing compassion for ourselves, our clients and our colleagues in the workplace, and restore us from some of the experiences we share.

Through learning from each other about practising compassion in health and social care, we can enhance our capacity to repair and protect the wellbeing of ourselves and colleagues, as well as promote good outcomes for clients and patients. Many of the authors spoke about their experiences of, or near misses with, burnout. Burnout was attributed to competing pressures at work, a strong desire to help others, and a self-focus on achieving and success. However, burnout could also be a force for change that resulted in doing things differently, changing one's approach and using what seems to be Snyder's (2000, 2002) concept of agency to find new pathways to overcome challenges when the consistent goal is to support people in their wellbeing. Throughout the three phases of the book, practising compassion, adopting compassion in life and sharing compassion with others, three key themes, or patterns, materialised:

1. **Compassionate curiosity and awareness of our selves**, considers the impact of shared compassion upon the parts of ourselves and how our different needs influence our capacity for hope and resilience in various circumstances. For instance, some of the particularly vulnerable parts of the self, such as the self-critic and our living memories of childhood stress experiences, are likely to need the enhanced support of the compassionate-self at times, which can often be nurtured and enhanced through shared compassion with another.

2. **Cultivating light in the shadows of illness and distress** explores the benefits and difficulties of practising shared compassion and self-kindness in practice, where there are often many external influences that can get in the way. However, creating space in advance for challenge and uncertainty, using our 'new brain's' abilities for imagination and planning, we can restore hopeful pathways and agency and benefit from vicarious hopefulness and resilience until we can re-establish our own.

3. **Cultivating wholeness with compassion** considers how nurturing a sense of togetherness through recognising our different needs and our *need to need* with others, allowing the 'helper' to share compassion too, can open new doors to hopeful outcomes and how to get there. Through experiencing vicarious resilience and borrowing hopeful agency from others, determination and hopefulness can be reignited and nurtured through self-compassion.

Compassionate curiosity and awareness of our *selves*

The concepts of multiple 'selves' within each of us has become a very natural one to me over recent years for various reasons. First, because I have been lucky enough to undertake research with people who kindly shared their stories with me about their experience of having different parts or alter states, diagnostically known as dissociative identity disorder[1] (Parry, Lloyd and Simpson 2016). The experience of doing this research was powerful for a number of reasons, although perhaps one of the most interesting findings was that communication with the younger child parts of the overall *self* was crucial in whether the threat system could be communicated with and soothed. For example, some participants described instances in which they continued to feel under threat and experience high levels of stress in situations that their adult parts could rationalise and manage but their child part(s) found difficult to understand, which would result in the person as a whole feeling stressed and exhausted.

Another reason that exploring experiences in terms of parts of the self seems so natural to me is that I have always felt quite aware of how people, and myself at times, compartmentalise. Even at a young age, I remember having conversations that started 'part of me thinks…' or 'part of me feels…'. I also remember looking around me and seeing how people acted very differently in particular situations. The multi-self work within compassionate mind training (e.g. Gilbert and Procter 2006) is often especially powerful, as people start to look at where certain thoughts and feelings come from and what previous, often childhood or relational experiences, underpin those reactions. Some parts of ourselves may find certain situations particularly stressful and threatening, which means we may need a little extra care at those times. For instance, in Chapters 8 and 9, Simone Bol and Jenny Shuttleworth Davies consider the role of the *young self* within educational contexts. Simone considers whether the means with which a young person coped with threat and fear as a child influences how they cope with challenges now around 'bigger powerful doing knowing' people. Further, Jenny discusses how stress starts early in schools, often with teachers modelling stress responses as they too feel the pressure to 'perform' vicariously through their young students. Are we then conditioned to respond with the 'drive/threat' system when faced with stress in the learning and work environments from an early age? Could our early life relationship with performance, stress and striving lead us to respond in a particular way as we age? Perhaps communicating with that younger, vulnerable and stressed part of ourselves and colleagues in these times could offer a new platform upon which to develop new pathways to success, with collegiate planning and problem solving enhancing the collective *agency* towards solutions and resolution. Given the vulnerability

---

1   See International Society for the Study of Trauma and Dissociation (2011) for further information.

of the health and social care systems in the UK at present, there seems no more urgent time than now to work in this way.

In her capacity as a healthcare professional, educator and doctoral trainee, Simone uses her unique position to reflect upon the impact of the higher education system upon a person's sense of self, ability and agency. She discusses how the *newness* of a hierarchical environment and the positioning of being at the start of a new journey can influence perceived agency, resources and empowerment. Particularly exploring how shame can grow without connection, she considers that when failures and disappointments are hidden from others, connection becomes disconnection and isolation leads to a loss of belongingness. Within a compassion framework, drawing upon Paul Gilbert's three emotion states, Simone reflects upon how a drive 'to do and know' and a threat from expectation 'to do *or* know' can leave a person feeling without agency or options: an 'infant-like state related to not knowing, being new, not knowing the environment and feeling powerless is generally particularly salient at the beginning of a new educational experience'. In this scenario, it seems to be the absence of agency for hopefulness that is most connected to powerlessness, which can perhaps transcend to any number of environments, such as starting a new training course, starting a new job, embarking on therapy as a client for the first time, working in a new setting and so on. It seems particularly important for practitioners to be aware of these processes and to educate service managers and clinical leaders around the importance of nurturing hopefulness, to enhance cognitive abilities and positive perceptions of oneself and others, fostering a safe and secure base to explore newness.

As a clinical psychologist working systemically with children, their families and colleagues from various disciplines, Kirsten Atherton discusses how offering nurture, warmth and acceptance to parents and colleagues in potentially distressing and unsettling situations can enhance trust in relationships and a safer approach to caring for a child. Through recognising the role of compassion in supporting the people within a system around a child and the particular vulnerabilities they may be experiencing, such as shame or anxiety, compassionate wisdom can create a protected space and safe base to explore possible options for going forward. This is another example of the link between hope and resilience: a practitioner can nurture a sense of agency and resilience in others, witness their approach and collaboratively move towards a mutually desired outcome.

Also within some of the narratives of this book are discussions of the *selves* that have different functions. Paul Gilbert's writings and teachings on compassionate mind training and compassion-focused therapy are incredibly helpful in facilitating greater understanding around how the parts of ourselves can work quite interdependently at times with or against each other, for example feeling cross with ourselves about feeling anxious or anxious about feeling anger. Equally, one of the most transformational moments in the compassionate mind training groups I have been involved with is when we explore multi-selves and the realisations people often share about their frightened, angry self and their protective, anxious self and the tenacity of their self-critic who usually only wants the best for them. It is these moments that let compassion flow through the whole self, mistakes, flaws and all.

Through greater awareness and knowledge of these processes, it becomes increasingly possible to appreciate the self-critic, as Liz Tallentire, Hannah Wilson, Ciara Joyce and I have explained in our personal reflections. It also highlights that alternative, healthy, long-term and sustainable strategies are needed, which can emerge from familiarisation and strengthening the compassionate-self, so relationships and health don't suffer. Although not explicitly stated, in her chapter, Mary Prendergast reflects upon how appreciative enquiry and reflective questioning can nurture curiosity and compassion for oneself and others, perhaps particularly the self-critic, which she connects to finding enhanced meaning, purpose and satisfaction in her work.

The role and power of the self-critic was discussed in various forms through the chapters. Discussing the role of the developing professional identity and the process of 'becoming what one is not already', Simone connects the processes of hope and striving and how the education system can trigger threat, sometimes creating a sense of powerlessness and hopelessness. In such situations, Simone proposes that a safety behaviour may be to let the internal self-critic become more powerful, thereby prohibiting a powerful 'other' from externally criticising. Importantly, Simone discusses how presenting ourselves as a 'finished, polished product' can hide the *human messiness of becoming* and perhaps portray a false sense of wholeness. Although we as educators can talk about 'continued learning', it is perhaps by sharing our failures as a natural part of the process, rather than something unfortunate that happened once that we mysteriously and quietly recovered from, that could add reality and authenticity to the narrative of shared experience – perhaps an example of vicarious resilience in education and learning. A great example of this is Hannah and Ciara's chapter, in which they humorously and honestly discuss their experiences of sharing being human, not perfect, which enhanced their mutual understanding and togetherness in the process of 'becoming': 'self-compassion is also committing to do our best for ourselves and accepting the responsibility for the challenges this endeavour brings'. Their story of the development of their 'imperfect-self' provides another glimpse of the fragmented ways in which we develop, with parts of ourselves, such as the self-critic, being nurtured from an early age, whereas other selves may need a little more encouragement to join the party later on.

Cultivating light in the shadows of illness and distress

When practised, self-compassion has been found to support emotional resilience in the face of adversity, as it disengages the threat system in favour of the caring system (Gilbert and Procter 2006). One of the reasons I enjoy sharing the power of compassion and self-kindness with my postgraduate students who work in health and social care is because it makes so much sense. Once I have introduced the group to the evolutionary physiology and evidence base behind the approach, including the need for strengthening the parasympathetic autonomic nervous system and the incredible power of the vagus nerve on our physical functioning and wellbeing (see Stellar *et al.* 2015 for a persuasive example), it seems almost silly not to try out the approach and become familiar with putting the exercises and philosophy into practice. Further, compassionate mind training for healthcare practitioners has been linked to enhanced empathy, psychological flexibility, searching for the values of our clients (discussed explicitly in Chapters 5 and 6 of this book), self-kindness and resilience (Seppala *et al.* 2014).

However, in acute health and social care settings where emotional energy, time and resources are increasingly scarce, where practitioners feel scrutinised by 'powerful others' (Delbanco and Bell 2007) and distress and uncertainty are certain (Ballatt and Campling 2011; de Zulueta, 2013), it is not surprising that the 'threat' system can take hold. Let's return for a moment to the work of Paquita de Zulueta (2015). Helpfully, de Zulueta differentiates between *emotional empathy*, which is the experience of feeling an emotional state with another – a shared emotional experience – and *cognitive empathy*: 'the ability for perspective taking and for imagining what it is like for the other person(s)' (de Zulueta 2015, p.3).

From a compassionate growth perspective, the difference is crucial, as 'feeling with' is a physiologically and psychologically different experience than the 'new brain' approach of 'imagining for', which offers professional distance whilst still creating space for compassion and hopefulness. When we consider this important difference in empathic response within the sometimes emotionally threatening environments we may work in, it becomes even clearer why we need to be mindful of the impact of these responses. In essence, the threat system (our *fight, flight, freeze* system) is our survival mode, which promotes self-focus and diminishes connection and compassion for others. Unaware and overactive emotionally empathic responses to the distress of others can lead to over-identification and further threat, thus ultimately creating a platform for disconnection. However, *cognitive empathy* can offer a useful alternative, through which the use of compassionate mind tools such as imagining, perspective taking and meaningful but professional connection can offer a space for hopeful agency and problem solving. Many critics of the current political climate surrounding healthcare, particularly in the UK, have emphasised the point that practitioners cannot be expected to maintain their hopefulness and resilience when under constant and consistent threat. In her discussion of the leadership needs within healthcare, de Zulueta proposes: 'Self-compassion is a key ingredient for resilience and the sustainability of compassion' (2015, p.4).

Based on my experiences and understanding from colleagues' stories, I propose that just as bees can't fly in heavy rain, just as flowers can't photosynthesise in darkness, hope and resilience cannot thrive without compassion. Experiences of bouncing back support personal agency, imagination fuels new pathways towards goals and further hopefulness, and compassionate connection underpins it all. Over time and with experience to practise, succeed, fail, and try again, compassionate acceptance of what is, compassionate growth around what may yet be and compassionate practice become possible.

Practising compassion in the workplace, in light of these organisational and political threats as well as the day-to-day pressures that many health and social care practitioners will be all too familiar with, seems crucial. In her chapter discussing her work as a clinical psychologist in a child and adolescent mental health service, Kirsten talks about the impact of using compassion to support colleagues to recognise and contain anxiety and frustration. She also highlights the many benefits for the staff team, parents/carers and young person of compassionately considering the wider system around a child and focusing on systemic need(s) to encourage wellbeing, thus using compassion to enhance understanding and accountability of a wider system. In Chapter 3, which considers compassion from the perspectives of psychologists in the UK and Malawi, Ndumanene Devlin Silungwe, a Malawian psychologist and therapist, proposes that professional empathy, similar to the Euro–American concept of cognitive empathy, can offer a level of disengagement to preserve practitioner wellbeing: 'empathy as a protective shield against getting overwhelmed'. Caroline Wyatt, a British clinical psychologist, reflects upon how empathy is encouraged in UK services, perhaps too uniformly. In a much more collectivist culture such as Devlin describes, where empathy can often mean the 'total immersion' in another's experiences (perhaps an extended form of emotional empathy), this approach can 'potentially avoid a rescuing dynamic' and 'reduce emotional burden on the clinician…by creating safe distance in the therapeutic relationship, without losing empathy'. Therefore, this appears to be an important culturally adaptive approach to self-care, as well as another reminder of the individualistic culture we in Western Europe work in. Whenever I stumble across reminders such as this, I am eternally grateful to the people in Romania, Bulgaria and India who shared their stories, experiences and homes with me in my teens and twenties. I learnt so much about myself and others in that time, perhaps no lesson as important as that a view of one should never eclipse the needs of the many.

As Director of Nursing at St Patrick's Hospital in Ireland, Mary has a rich and varied knowledge of implementing self-care and the impact of reflection, self-acceptance and gratitude. Mary discusses her gratitude for being able to serve others, with an emphasis on the need for care providers to be secure in their own wellbeing and ability to provide compassion for themselves and others, to create 'healing moments of engagement [that] support compassionate practice'. Through her work as an educator in healthcare practice, Mary illustrates her chapter with examples of how 'compassion is a lived value'. In relation to managing anxiety and distress in the workplace, Mary focuses on the interpersonal relationships between carer and patient, recognising that hardships (or storms) are often a part of the renewal and restorative processes that we experience as practitioners. Such stories of struggle that result in a change in perspective, behaviour, direction or focus are reminiscent of the aforementioned connection between hope and resilience, supported by compassionate practices. Both Liz and Sarah Lawson discuss how their times of difficulty, failure and burnout led them to find a new pathway to their ultimate goals, which fostered their hopefulness and restored agency and ability to manage distress.

For Liz, her prior experiences of observing hardship and struggle in the lives of others facilitated an internalised, genuine, non-judgemental and compassionately accepting mindset for her clinical practice and her own struggles in difficult times. Liz's new approach of living with compassion and taking self-compassion out of a professional self and into her personal life seemed to offer new pathways to hope and resilience, to frame failure as a normal part of life's rich journey. Liz's story also offers a further example of the cyclical nature of hope and resilience, as she discusses developing resilience as a result of difficult experiences, which she now sees as facilitating greater empathy and understanding towards others, possibly cultivating shared hopefulness through the shared humanity of living through hardships and embracing struggle. Although experiences offer a platform to develop resilience and hopeful pathways, and agency paves the way to determination, it seems that looking back on those experience with self-kindness can operationalise new hope for the future and expand horizons in terms of what may be possible in the future, enhancing hope and enriching resilience. What matters too is how we cope with them and maintain our wellbeing in preparation for what comes next.

In the final chapter, Jenny discusses how the NHS has become a business, designed to do what it was never meant for in a technological, social and political climate that could not have been anticipated, becoming a hostile place for caring people to work. She highlights that the language of shame is often used to motivate people towards success, although we know from the work of many academics and practitioners, particularly shame researcher Brené Brown (2012) to whom Jenny originally introduced me, that shaming does little to influence behaviour change in the end: 'Shame is a focus on self, guilt is a focus on behaviour.' Jenny also highlights that the current UK health system is far removed from the foundation of kinship and a notion of safety through belongingness, which the NHS was originally built upon. Further, a recurring theme through the chapters of this book and wider publications demonstrates that nurturing hopefulness through heartfelt connection in caring relationships promotes a more positive experience for all involved and a shared hopefulness, which can nurture resilience in the face of adversity. If we as 'carers' allow ourselves to be 'trained out' of compassion, there will be consequences at individual, relational and organisational levels. Simone highlights the shared humanity in group contexts and the importance of community and belonging: 'similarities and differences in emotional experiences are enhancing and supportive and provide a rich experience of humanity.'

With a specific focus upon the compassionate growth within the 'becoming professional self', Sarah and Kirsten make two particularly relevant points in relation to this process. First, Sarah reflects that *striving* driven by the self-critic can be effective in some ways, although it makes us less courageous about trying new things for fear of failure and not being good enough. She discusses the power of visualising possible futures to help turn up the volume on self-compassion. To me, this seems to directly link compassionate mind practices to Snyder's Hope Theory (e.g. 2000, 2002) in that Sarah talks about visualising new possibilities, i.e. possible pathways using the imagery powers of the evolved 'new brain' (see Gilbert 2010, p.6), to promote agency in one's abilities so as to move closer to the desired goal. Second, Kirsten brings accountability to the fore in considering how and why we should tone up our practitioner self-compassion to counterbalance the *strive*. Kirsten discusses the need for practitioners to take responsibility for making time for self-care and using compassionate wisdom to 'check in' on whether we're doing it: 'It is helpful to plan in slippage for processing time and unplanned duty or crisis work.' If there is one thing we can expect in our line of work, it is the unexpected. However, by taking the advice on board to plan in 'slippage' and tune in to the life we actually have rather than an idealised working life with certainty and predictability, we can still ensure we have room for implementing the self-care and time for reflection that we know our *professional self* requires to maintain a capacity for continued compassionate growth.

> *Compassion is an expression and commitment in the working environment.*
> *It is a key in relationships or projects.*
>
> Mary Prendergast

Interestingly, most of the chapters at one point or another discuss the internal and external threats to practising compassion, particularly self-compassion. The processes discussed amongst the chapters in relation to the threats, drives and soothing nature of practising compassion in professional practice and developing compassionate growth are summarised in Figure P4.1, in an adapted version of Paul Gilbert's three types of emotional regulation system. Despite the difficulties associated with practising compassion at times in certain environments, many of the authors indicated that with the right support and a commitment to 'becoming' and nurturing self-compassion and compassion for others, hope can often come from an acceptance of doing the best one can rather than flawless success alone.

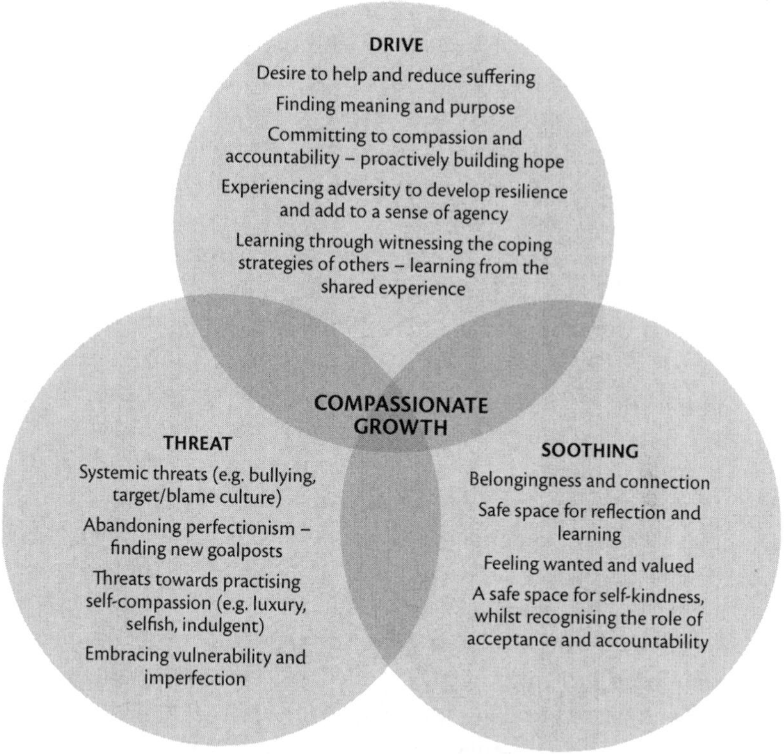

DRIVE

Desire to help and reduce suffering

Finding meaning and purpose

Committing to compassion and accountability – proactively building hope

Experiencing adversity to develop resilience and add to a sense of agency

Learning through witnessing the coping strategies of others – learning from the shared experience

COMPASSIONATE GROWTH

THREAT

Systemic threats (e.g. bullying, target/blame culture)

Abandoning perfectionism – finding new goalposts

Threats towards practising self-compassion (e.g. luxury, selfish, indulgent)

Embracing vulnerability and imperfection

SOOTHING

Belongingness and connection

Safe space for reflection and learning

Feeling wanted and valued

A safe space for self-kindness, whilst recognising the role of acceptance and accountability

Figure P4.1 The development of compassionate growth for the professional self, adapted from Gilbert's emotional regulation systems model

Cultivating wholeness with compassion

As we approach the end of this book, now seems a good time to bring our deconstructions of stories, concepts and the *selves* together. Within the chapters, there are many examples of how compassion can lead to unity, togetherness and wholeness. For instance, Liz described the experience of compassion as a deep empathy, more than only a cognitive process but a full body experience, although highlights that this can be positive for therapeutic relationships but costly in terms of energy for the practitioner. Rehabilitation Consultant and Occupational Therapist, Edith Macintosh, discusses her experiences of a *strong heart response* to the suffering of others and how, like Mary, she tries to be guided by the values of her patients to find *what* and *who* matters to them to foster meaning and hope – perhaps by expanding their hopeful pathways and agency through sharing resources and vicarious resilience. Edith also explains how her work offers her fulfilment and satisfaction from serving others. To illustrate this, Edith offers the example of a practitioner's drive of wanting to alleviate suffering in another, which would also trigger discomfort in themselves through imagining or vicariously experiencing distress through an empathic response, being soothed by their own action – resulting in the shared healing of both the client and carer through their connection. She reflects that: 'Compassion may not always be comfortable or for comfort', although seemingly by considering 'compassion' as both a verb and emotion, the 'doing' impacts the 'feelings' of all involved. In this way, 'walking that hard road with them' and appreciating the shared and dynamic nature of compassion facilitates its restorative nature.

Considering wholeness and togetherness in this manner also reminds me of the ways in which we can implement our knowledge of and benefit from vicarious resilience (Hernández, Gangsei and Engstrom 2007). Whilst conducting a recent review around the impact of talking therapies for adult survivors of childhood sexual abuse (Parry and Simpson 2016), I was struck by the power of vicarious trauma and resilience in some of the therapeutic groups explored. Although some people reported hearing the harrowing stories of others as being highly distressing and triggering for their own traumatic experiences, others looked to the other side of the story, to the ending, to seek a hopeful end through the stories of others that they were struggling to find for themselves.

Similarly, in a compassionate mind training group I was involved in last year, one of the participants explained that the multi-self exercises in the group had helped her unearth certain experiences and responses to increase her sense of self-understanding and wholeness: 'you're gonna see sides of you that you didn't know you had and that may possibly be helpful because…that's when we're starting to understand' (Merry in Parry and Malpus, 2017 p.10). Through the narratives offered in this book and through discussions with colleagues and students who explore the uses of shared compassion, it seems that compassionate acceptance and self-compassion are the keys to enhancing a sense of wholeness – creating a safe space in which no parts of the self feel the need to react or feel threatened on their own. The experience of sharing compassion with others and ourselves, and letting ourselves be open to having compassion shared with us (even if it is uncomfortable to some *selves* such as the self-critic), can operationalise hope and resilience for us at home and at work, enhancing our wellbeing through connection.

Guideposts for sharing compassion: fostering hope and resilience in practice

1. Borrowing hopeful agency from others, helping us believe 'we can do it' even when we may be doubtful of our abilities, can enhance our faith in our chosen course of action towards a desired goal.

2. Recognising that we are often not united whole selves but a collection of experiences in time and responses to those experiences, which can make some parts of ourselves feel particularly vulnerable in various environments, may be important in recognising our need to need and need for shared compassion.

3. Looking for examples of how others succeed and overcome struggle, through leaning on vicarious resilience when our own ability to see a way to bounce back from adversity is under threat, can create new pathways towards our targets and hopes. Letting in shared compassion, even when that may be a little threatening to some parts of ourselves, can enhance our capacity for self-kindness, soothing space and potential for hope.

4. Embracing compassionate acceptance can nurture hope and resilience in a shared compassionate space, allowing togetherness with others without hierarchies and with recognising the messiness of being human.

References

Ballatt, J. and Campling, P. (2011). *Intelligent Kindness: Reforming the Culture of Healthcare.* London: The Royal College of Psychiatrists Publications.

Brown, B. (2012). *Listening to Shame* [TED talk]. Available at www.ted.com/talks/brene_brown_listening_to_shame, accessed on 21 February 2017.

Delbanco, T. and Bell, S. K. (2007). Guilty, afraid, and alone – struggling with medical error. *The New England Journal of Medicine, 357*(17), 1682.

Gilbert, P. (2010). *Training Our Minds in, with and for Compassion. An Introduction to Concepts and Compassion-Focused Exercises.* Available at http://wtm.thebreathproject.org/wp-content/uploads/2016/03/COMPASSION-HANDOUT.pdf, accessed on 21 February 2017.

Gilbert, P. and Procter, S. (2006). Compassionate mind training for people with high shame and self-criticism: Overview and pilot study of a group therapy approach. *Clinical Psychology and Psychotherapy, 13*(6), 353–379.

Hernández, P., Gangsei, D. and Engstrom, D. (2007). Vicarious resilience: A new concept in work with those who survive trauma. *Family Process, 46*(2), 229–241.

International Society for the Study of Trauma and Dissociation (2011). Guidelines for treating dissociative identity disorder in adults, third revision. *Journal of Trauma and Dissociation, 12*(2), 115–187.

Kapoulitsas, M. and Corcoran, T. (2015). Compassion fatigue and resilience: A qualitative analysis of social work practice. *Qualitative Social Work, 14*(1), 86–101.

Krasner, M. S., Epstein, R. M., Beckman, H., Suchman, A. L. *et al.* (2009). Association of an educational program in mindful communication with burnout, empathy and attitudes among primary care physicians. *JAMA, 302*(12), 1284–1293.

Parry, S., Lloyd, M. and Simpson, J. (2016) Experiences of therapeutic relationships on hospital wards, dissociation and making connections. *Journal of Trauma and Dissociation.* Available at www.tandfonline.com/doi/full/10.1080/15299732.201 6.1241852, accessed on 21 February 2017.

Parry, S. and Simpson, J. (2016). How do adult survivors of childhood sexual abuse experience formally delivered talking therapy? A systematic review. *Journal of Child Sexual Abuse, 25*(7), 793–812.

Parry, S. and Malpus, Z. (2017). Reconnecting the mind and Body: A pilot study of developing compassion for persistent pain. *Patient Experience Journal, 4*(1), 145–153.

Raab, K. (2014). Mindfulness, self-compassion, and empathy among health care professionals: A review of the literature. *Journal of Health Care Chaplaincy, 20*(3), 95–108.

Seppala, E., Hutcherson, C., Nguyen, D., Doty, J. and Gross, J. (2014). Loving-kindness meditation: A tool to improve healthcare provider compassion, resilience, and patient care. *Journal of Compassionate Health Care, 1*(1), 9–9.

Snyder, C. R. (2000). *Handbook of Hope Theory, Measures and Applications.* San Diego, CA: Academic Press.

Snyder, C. R. (2002). Hope theory: Rainbows of the mind. *Psychological Inquiry, 13*(4), 249–275.

Stellar, J. E., Cohen, A., Oveis, C. and Keltner, D. (2015). Affective and physiological responses to the suffering of others: Compassion and vagal activity. *Journal of Personality and Social Psychology, 108*(4), 572–585.

de Zulueta P. (2013) Compassion in 21st century medicine: Is it sustainable? *Clinical Ethics, 8*(4) 87–90, 119–128.

de Zulueta, P. (2015). Developing compassionate leadership in health care: An integrative review. *Journal of Healthcare Leadership, 2016*(8), 1–10.

Further Reading and Resources

Ali Miller's website: Befriending Ourselves – Resources for Inner Peace and Compassionate Self-care: www.befriendingourselves.com

Brené Brown's film about empathy: www.youtube.com/watch?v=1Evwgu369Jw

Michael Margolis at TEDxFurmanU: The stories we choose to live: www.youtube.com/watch?v=fwlT6eUpTNM

Workplace wellbeing: www.mind.org.uk/workplace/mental-health-at-work/taking-care-of-yourself/five-ways-to-wellbeing

Brené Brown, Researcher and Storyteller, 'Maybe stories are just data with a soul': http://brenebrown.com

Innovation and proactivity around wellbeing: www.wellbeingenterprises.org.uk

A wonderful space for women of all stages: www.wellbeingofwomen.org.uk

Self-Compassion, Kristin Neff, 'With self-compassion, we give ourselves the same kindness and care we'd give to a good friend': http://self-compassion.org

Contributors

Sarah Parry is a senior lecturer at Manchester Metropolitan University in England, UK and a practising clinical psychologist with a residential looked-after children's service in Manchester. Sarah's research interests include therapeutic uses of formulation, the therapeutic utility of compassion in practice for clients and practitioners, exploring the lived experiences of people who experience dissociation and the coping mechanisms of young people who have experienced abuse and neglect.

Simone Bol works as a senior lecturer at Manchester Metropolitan University where she currently teaches Speech and Language Therapy students in the areas of clinical linguistics and applied psychology. Simone worked clinically for many years providing assessment and intervention for children and adults with a variety of communication difficulties, and supporting adults and children with mental health difficulties in secure, open and community settings. She is currently completing a doctorate in Counselling Psychology and practises as a trainee Counselling Psychologist at Mind and Just Psychology CIC. Simone has a focus on working with diversity, including neurodiversity and cultural and linguistic diversity. She is particularly interested in the areas of language and identity, from a clinical and academic perspective, and has engaged in advanced academic study in linguistics and social sciences. She also has a special interest in learning from experience as well as academic learning and in investigating the relationships between these areas of learning. Compassion is a constant inspiration and aspiration in all areas of her work.

Jenny Shuttleworth Davies works as a clinical tutor on the Lancaster University DClinPsy training programme. She leads the 'Personal

Development and Reflection' teaching strand and has facilitated compassionate mind groups with trainee clinical psychologists over the last five years. Her clinical and research interests include attachment theory and the perinatal period. She is also chair of the Sharing Stories group, an international collaboration aiming to improve emotional wellbeing in both Ugandan and UK communities.

Edith Macintosh has a background in healthcare and is a qualified occupational therapist and has many years experience as a clinician and service manager. Since 2009 she has worked in the Care Inspectorate in Scotland. Edith initially worked as the Rehabilitation Consultant leading national improvement initiatives for the social care sector, in partnership with different organisations to improve the lives of people using care services. In January 2017 Edith was appointed Head of Improvement Support and now leads the improvement activity for the organisation to drive forward improvement in social care and social work across Scotland. Edith is passionate about people's rights and enabling everyone to participate, contribute and enjoy life to the full no matter their situation or ability.

Ciara Joyce is a final year trainee on the Doctorate in Clinical Psychology at Lancaster University. She is interested in fostering holistic and sustainable approaches to wellbeing, which consider service users and practitioners as people working alongside one another in the imperfect pursuit of health and happiness. Ciara believes self-compassion lies at the core of this process, and feels that much of her training has involved revelling in the many challenges to putting this into practice.

Kirsten Atherton has worked in child and family physical and mental health services in several locations around the north west of England and the west of Scotland. Kirsten qualified as a clinical psychologist through the doctoral training at the University of Liverpool. Kirsten learnt how to use compassion focused methods through completing the introductory training taught by Dr Mary Welford in 2013. Kirsten found this inspiring and a natural fit to her existing outlook, and thus has been trying to adopt the approach both in clinical practice, and life more broadly, ever since.

Sarah Lawson is a chartered clinical psychologist and coaching psychologist, and an ICF Accredited Coach. Sarah works in an integrative and creative way, bringing a whole-person approach to her work. Sarah has more than 15 years' experience in psychology, mental health and wellbeing. Her areas of research interests are in compassion fatigue, post-traumatic growth and resilience. She has worked in both the NHS and private sector in the UK and Middle East.

Mary Prendergast is the Director of Nursing in St Patrick's Hospital, Cashel, Co Tipperary. For the last 16 years Mary has acted locally, regionally and nationally on service users' participation in health service developments. She is responsible for the first (SUF) public service users group facilitated in Ireland and located in South Tipperary. Mary has contributed and presented extensively over the years on the Patient Participation Principal. Mary specialises in training of nursing and support staff, and service users in quality programmes, practice development and organisational change. Presently Mary is teaching through the Regional Centre for Nursing and Midwifery Education Unit. Mary is a Human Givens Counsellor with a specific an interest and practice in debriefing and has completed programmes in psychology, psychotherapy and coaching.

Liz Tallentire is a clinical psychologist, a mother, a mindfulness teacher, and a scuba diver. She has her own private clinical psychology practice and works in the NHS. She is particularly interested in therapy and research related to attachment relationships and emotion regulation. She has publications of her qualitative participatory research in the *Journal of Applied Research in Intellectual Disabilities* and the conference proceedings of the 13th International Conference on the Care & Treatment of Offenders with a Learning Disability. Her thesis 'Psychological factors related to epileptic and non-epileptic seizures' included a quantitative empirical study incorporating attachment, emotion regulation and trauma.

Hannah Wilson is a qualified clinical psychologist who works in both the NHS and independent practice. She has a keen interest in personal and professional development. Hannah continues to pursue her own understanding of compassion, and applying it in 'real life' – it's something of a work in progress!

Caroline Wyatt, Olivia Wadham and Amy D'Sa are clinical psychologists from the UK who met whilst completing their Doctorate in Clinical Psychology at Lancaster University. During their studies they each developed an interest in issues around global mental health and spent time exploring these whilst working in Malawi and Uganda. They first met Devlin (who is one of very few clinical psychologists based in Malawi) in 2014 and have worked together to develop placement opportunities for trainee psychologists in Malawi. Caroline, Olivia and Amy are the founding trustees of a charity called The Umoza Trust which develops international links between mental health services with a view to learning from each other.

Subject Index

Author Index